TALES FROM THE
CITY

TALES FROM THE
CITY

A collection of writing inspired
by Norwich City Football Club

Volume Three
Edited by Mick Dennis

TALES FROM
www.talesfrom.com

First published in Great Britain in 2017
by Tales From

Printed and bound by Page Bros Ltd

Visual design by www.stonecreativedesign.com
Cover typography and additional design by Steve Leard

ISBN 978-0-9932381-5-4

Tales From Ltd
107 Jupiter Drive, Hemel Hempstead, Herts HP2 5NU
Registered company number: 9082738

www.talesfrom.com
info@talesfrom.com

TALES FROM THE CITY

CONTENTS

INTRODUCTION

BY THE EDITOR

Towards the end of the 2016-17 campaign, there was much online discussion among Norwich City fans about who should be the player of the season. As is often the way with Internet chatter, things became over-heated rapidly.

The bone of contention was whether Wes Hoolahan should win. Those who were going to vote for him included many who argued — and 'argued' quickly became the apposite word — that there might not be another opportunity to give the award to Wessi. We should make sure the little genius got his hands on the Barry Butler Trophy before it was too late, they said.

That thinking outraged some City supporters. 'It's not a lifetime's achievement award. It's player of the season', they insisted, often with shouty capital letters and, before long, with expletives.

For me, it was straightforward. Everyone can vote for anyone. The award goes to the bloke who gets the most votes. That's it.

But the online dispute raged on. One quarrel involved two guys I know. I like them both. But they became more and more rude about each other. Think about that: two Norwich fans, decent chaps, having such a pointless yet impassioned squabble — bickering like Saturday night drunks on Prince of Wales Road.

I chose Wes — because Mrs Dennis has a thing about him. He won, even the rowdiest rows subsided, and I do understand that every club has daft internecine spats. But I think they've become nastier and more frequent thanks to the Internet —

which is like a toilet wall for which everyone has a felt-tip pen. Consider the club in Suffolk. Before the Internet, what were the chances of two members of their tiny fan base bumping into each other to have a shouting match?

In the fine city, post-match debates used to end as soon as Canary Call gave way to ancient pop tunes. But now conflicts can be revived online after months, sometimes years. And since the *Pink Un* message board ceased being moderated, it is certainly not moderate. It is not restrained by any sense that we're all on the same side.

But we most definitely are. And I hope this book reminds readers that we foot soldiers in the Yellow Army have far too much in common to be fighting among ourselves. Some might scream support from the Snake Pit. Some of us might sit with a more studious air in the Community Upper. But even if we are diagonally opposite each other at Carrow Road, we are not diametrically opposed. We care, far too deeply probably, about the same football club. And I think we care so much because doing so gives us a sense of identity: of belonging and believing, of hoping and fearing... together.

So my wish is that this book will add to the fund of shared Norwich City experiences. I want to introduce some fans and re-introduce others to people who have written the history of our club with their deeds. And I want the Tales of four fans, who took very diverse routes before finding themselves at home at Carrow Road, to demonstrate that, for all our differences, we are united. Well, no, we're City, but you know what I mean.

There is one Tale that I need to explain. Duncan Forbes is not well enough these days to sit down and write his story. But not very many years ago Rick Waghorn interviewed him for a chapter in a book that was never published. I had to fillet out Rick's description of places and events so that I was left only with Duncan's words. With the blessing of his wife, Janette, I then nursed those words into a narrative account.

I did so with the utmost affection, and I'd had some practice. At the height of his Norwich City fame, I used to help Duncan with *The Captain's Column* each week in the *Pink Un*.

In that long-ago era, Duncan decided one summer that he needed to keep himself fit by slogging up and down the hills of Mousehold Heath (an area which was not entirely salubrious after dark). My then fiancée drove up to interview him, and her report for the *Norwich Mercury* was illustrated with a magnificent photograph, taken by Paul Hewitt. Rob Butler of BBC Radio Norfolk tweeted in 2017 that the picture, taken 40 years earlier, was his favourite Norwich City portrait of all time. It's mine too, and I am glad that it has been possible to reproduce it in this book because, with the city's skyline behind him as he runs, Duncan Forbes, a warrior captain who led the team to new heights, looks every inch the Mr Norwich he is.

© Archant Norfolk

Six months after that truly iconic image was created, Duncan announced that he did not want me to help him with his *Captain's Column* that week. When I returned to work after my honeymoon, I saw what he had put at the conclusion of that column. 'Congratulations to *Pink Un* writer Mick Dennis who was married today. I once met his bride on Mousehold Heath and she seemed very nice.'

So the editor's acknowledgements for this book begin with my wife, Sarah, whose love has been constant down the subsequent decades — her love for Norwich City.

Thanks are also due to David 'Spud' Thornhill, whose offer to fact-check every chapter I accepted gratefully because I had already encountered his encyclopedic knowledge of our club.

Finally, I am indebted to four men: Rick Waghorn, Archant's Chris Lakey, former NCFC publications editor Peter Rogers and Joe Ferrari, the club's director of communications. Getting Duncan's Tale presented challenges that were only surmounted because those four instantly endorsed the idea. You see, they share my admiration for Duncan, and understand how important it is that other Norwich fans should read his words.

There can be no better illustration of what I want this book, and the others in the series, to help achieve: the Norwich City community coming together.

Mick Dennis

1

Norwich fans had a special song about **Simon Lappin** but, for one long period of his Carrow Road career, he had nothing to sing about. Here, for the first time, is his inside story of seven roller coaster seasons under five managers. It is a remarkable Tale of how he was signed by Peter Grant, ostracised by Glenn Roeder, rescued by Bryan Gunn, championed by Paul Lambert, sold by Chris Hughton — and adored by supporters.

BANISHED BUT NOT BROKEN

BY SIMON LAPPIN

I was brought up in Airdrie, 20 miles or so east of Glasgow — and about 1,500 miles north of the Royal Palace in Madrid. So not quite as Spanish as my complexion or the song Norwich fans sung about me would suggest. Norwich City gave me the absolute best of times and, for a spell, the worst of times, but I never thought I would end up having my own song.

Simon Lappin, King of Spain, King of Spain, King of Spain. Simon Lappin, King of Spain. He looks Spanish.

I jokingly tell people that my children don't know the words to 'London Bridge Is Falling Down' because they think the real words are the ones about their daddy, which I taught them. But, no, I really did grow up in Airdrie, with dad John, mum Esther and twin sisters, Loreen and Linsey, who are older than me. My dad had played a few games for the reserves at Hamilton Accies, but ours wasn't a particularly sporty household. My dad wanted me to go to uni and study to fulfil my ambition of becoming a pilot. It was my mum who thought I should take the football opportunity that had been offered to me — YTS forms with St Mirren — because, she said, I could always go back to education later. Mum and football won.

Believe it or not, I was a tricky, goal-scoring winger. I know my goals record as I got older would suggest otherwise, but I was. I was tiny, too. It wasn't until I was 15 or 16 that I shot up a bit.

To begin with at St Mirren I became spectacularly proficient at mopping floors — like all the YTS lads I had a lot of cleaning duties. But the football went well and I managed to represent my country at under-16, under-17, under-19 and under-21. By the time I got to the under-21s, Berti Vogts was manager of the national senior team and he had Rainer Bonhof as his under-21 coach. They were both World Cup winners and Rainer was an unbelievable coach.

My first under-21 call-up was in 2004, when Gus Macpherson had taken over at St Mirren. Gus's assistant was Andy Millen. If you played against this guy, you'd think he was an absolute psychopath, but he became a teammate and a really good friend off the pitch. To this day he is the person in the game who I trust the most and always turn to for advice.

In the 2005-06 season I scored in the Bells Scottish Cup Final, when St Mirren beat a Hamilton Academical side including Alex Neil, and then we followed that up by finishing top of the second tier to win promotion to the Scottish Premier League.

But, whenever the press asked me about my ambitions, I told them I wanted to play in England. I played more than 170 times for St Mirren, but when we won the First Division, our average attendance was under 5,000 and there were teams in the league with averages of less than 1,000. Not quite the numbers I would eventually play in front of.

Norwich were the first English club to make a firm move for me. It was January 2007, a few days before my 24th birthday. You can't imagine how excited I was and the following Tuesday after training I got a flight from Glasgow to Stansted, and then a train to Norwich. I changed into my suit on the train in a toilet — which, if you've ever done, you'll know is not easy.

I arrived in Norwich just before the club's evening game against Wolves. As I turned the corner and saw the floodlights, and the crowds walking up to the ground, it gave me goose bumps. And I remember walking out into the directors' box to watch the game and getting that view, from the middle of the main stand, of the whole ground. It was full. I was absolutely blown away.

I signed and that Saturday we were at home to Leeds. Adam Drury, who was captain at the time, was suspended, so the manager said to me, 'Look I know you didn't come here to play in defence, but I'd like you to play left-back'.

So I said, 'Aye, no problem'.

I hadn't expected to go straight into the team, so I wasn't going to complain about where I was picked. My mum, dad, and my fiancée, Jill, came down for the game but couldn't get a flight. They wouldn't have missed my Norwich debut for the world so they set off from Airdrie at about four in the morning for the long drive down.

Practically the first thing I did was a slide-tackle, down near the River End, and I remember a huge roar from the crowd. Jonny Howson (yeah, *the* Jonny Howson) scored for them after about 20 minutes, but Dion Dublin equalised just before the hour and Darren Huckerby got the winner 11 minutes from the end.

Dion was playing centre-back, alongside me in the back four. Hucks was playing in front of me on the left — which meant I didn't see too much of him because he was too busy terrorising the Leeds defence — and I had to pinch myself thinking, 'These guys are my teammates now!'

At the finish, Dion picked me up and hugged me, almost squeezing the life out of me, and I won the sponsors' man of the match award. Ads came out of the tunnel at full time and said, 'Well done, mate. Superb'. That meant the absolute world to me.

I met up with my mum, dad and Jill and it was like, 'What just happened?' It was hard to process. The previous Saturday

I'd been in a beaten St Mirren side in front of 4,921. A week later I'd helped beat Leeds United in front of 25,018.

Jill moved south from Scotland and got a job with Lotus Cars, which she absolutely loved, and worked there until our children were born. Peter Grant was the manager who signed me, and his wife, Lorraine, was a massive help to Jill, making her feel welcome. Peter himself was always trying to make sure we were settling down OK. His PA, Val Lemmon, was practically my Norwich mum in my time at the club and her late husband, Trevor, was absolutely brilliant. Jill and I will be forever grateful to them as they were always prepared to help in any way they could.

The games came thick and fast in the Championship and I managed to keep my place in the team. Ads was recalled at left-back, and Hucks was still further forward on that left side and so I was playing on the left of central midfield in a sort of lop-sided 4-4-2. All I had to do was get the ball to Hucks!

My first goal was at Luton, in the February. Luton led twice but Chrissy Martin, who'd just got in the team, equalised after the first one and Jason Shackell got our second equaliser with about a quarter of an hour left. Right at the end, in added time, we got a free-kick. Youssef Safri and me stood over the ball. I'd been practising free-kicks after training, staying out so long and so often that the groundsmen were fed up with me. I said to Saff, 'I fancy this. It's on my side'. I managed to get the ball up, over the wall, and it sailed in.

It was quite an important goal. When I'd signed for Norwich I didn't even look where they were in the table, because it was such a big opportunity for me. But we'd been getting closer and closer to being dragged into the relegation fight and the win at Luton moved us away from it.

I had an operation on a broken thumb before the end of the season and missed four of the last five games, but when we came back for the pre-season after the summer I was probably fitter than I'd ever been in my career. I had to be because the club signed quite a lot of players in the summer, and some of them were more competition for me. Julien Brellier was bought from Hearts and Darel Russell was brought back from Stoke. Then, in the August, Ian Murray arrived from Rangers. So that was three who could play in midfield. I had to fight for my place.

We had a so-so start and, for whatever reason, it started to get worse. Sometimes you cannot put your finger on why you can't get out of a rut. And then losing becomes a habit, just like winning can be a habit. It was a terrible time.

In October, after losing 1-0 at QPR — their first home win of the season — Peter Grant resigned. I was gutted to see him go because he was the one who had signed me and I felt I had let him down.

Glenn Roeder took over. Ads had picked up an injury, so I played left-back again in the new manager's first game — a 2-2 draw at home to Ipswich. We were losing 2-0 at half-time but put together a good comeback and I was Sky's man of the match. So I was thinking, 'OK, we might get back on track under this guy and maybe I should play left-back more!' Everything seemed fine.

But then we played Watford at home in the midweek, and again I was left-back. We got beat 3-1 and it could have been 10-1. The next match was down in Plymouth. I can remember that Ian Murray had come into the team. He was really, and normally, a defender, but he was picked in left midfield. Me — normally a midfield man — I was at left-back. We lost 3-0. I was dropped for the next game, which I couldn't really complain about, although the manager hadn't seen me in my true position.

The next time we went in for training, one of the coaches pulled a few of the lads and told them they had to go and train with the youth team. I was one of them. There was no explanation or discussion. We were thinking it was maybe punishment for the poor performance on Saturday, but it was the start of a nightmare period for me at the club. The manager is paid to decide who plays, and if he had said to me from the start, 'Look, the last manager signed you but I want to go in a different direction'… well, I'd have said, 'Fair enough'. But there was no conversation. I was just cast aside.

After a few days of training away from the first-team, I asked to see him. He just said, 'You are not part of my plans, I don't want you here and I don't want you around my team'.

My world caved in. I thought, 'I worked for years to get to a club like Norwich, to play at this level, and you are going to take it away just like that…'.

He brought in a lot of loan players and so I knew that I was getting lower and lower in the pecking order — even if he had been prepared to consider me for selection, which he obviously wasn't. It was the worst time of my career.

In the following January, St Mirren phoned me and asked me to go back. They offered me a three-year contract and Gus MacPherson was still the manager. He had been great for me and hadn't wanted me to leave in the first place. But our home was in Norfolk by then, and I wasn't ready to give up on playing in England.

I know in football some people think, 'Oh, he's happy just picking up his money and doesn't care about not playing.' Well, in my case that was one million per cent untrue. It was never about money. There was talk of going to other clubs for the same money but I had only been at Norwich for a year, and I just didn't want to quit on a club I really liked.

I was so far from the first-team at Norwich, though, that I realised I probably had to go somewhere on loan. And, in the end, I went to Motherwell for four months. Mark McGhee was the manager and there was a great group of players. I was grateful for the opportunity to enjoy football again. We finished third behind Rangers and Celtic and I managed to score the only goal in a 1-0 win at Celtic Park, which gave me a massive lift. Mark said that he wanted me to come back for the following season. But I said, 'I appreciate the offer but I want to go back to Norwich'.

Mr Roeder didn't seem overjoyed to have me back. Norwich had stayed up and on the first day of pre-season, the players had medical tests. He walked by and said to me, 'I need to have a word with you'. I said, 'Yeah, I'd like a word too'.

I felt I had done well in my stint at Motherwell and even though I was back, ready to fight for a chance, part of me knew it wouldn't come with him at the helm. I needed a day off for my best mate's wedding and as I wasn't selected to travel for the first-team's trip to Sweden, I asked for it thinking it wouldn't be a problem. I said, 'If I can go to the wedding, I'll fly back to Norwich and train on the Sunday'.

But he said, 'Nah. You're not going to any wedding'.

I said, 'I'm the Best Man!'

Now, this wasn't exactly true. I was actually an usher. I couldn't see why he was being like that. I had to phone my best mate and apologise for not being able to make his wedding. Then the manager pulled me really late on the Friday afternoon and said, 'You can go to your mate's wedding'. I phoned my mate again and when I couldn't get a flight, I set a new land speed record driving back to Scotland — and it had all been so unnecessary.

The manager's next move a while later was to call me in and say, 'You are free to leave'. But I told him that I hadn't worked all those years to get the chance of playing at this level in England just to walk away.

Training with the kids every day was soul-destroying, though. When it comes to training and games, I can be a bit of a moaner. Ask any of the lads I've played with and they'll tell

you. It's the way I am. I can moan with the best of them — and
that's when things are going well! But things were not going
well and on occasion, I took my frustration out on the young
lads, which was unfair of me. But that's exactly what it was —
sheer frustration.

It was a bleak time. And at times it must have been hard for
Jill to see me miserable. She was unbelievable throughout it all.
I'd like to think I would be supportive if she needed me to be,
but I do know she was something special: amazing. She used
to come to watch reserve games. I would look up and see this
lonely figure sitting in the stand — the only member of the
Norwich City Reserves Away Supporters' Club.

One day at home it all got to me, and there were a few tears
shed. But I kept training with the kids — all week with no big
game on the Saturday. And it was the same the next week and
the next, and on it went.

On one occasion I was called over to play the role of an
opposition defender while the first-team were being coached.
I was supposed to be passive: just to take up position and not
really try to get to the ball. But I kept stepping in front of the
striker and getting it. The manager was showing the first-team
what he wanted. After I'd been decidedly non-passive a few
times, he came and started backing into me, as if he was the
striker. So the next time the ball came in, instead of letting it go
in behind me, as I was supposed to, I stepped in and cleared it
into the car-park. He had an absolute rage but I allowed myself
a cheeky smile.

But results weren't going very well and the boys were in
another rut. Suddenly the manager decided to have me training
with the first-team again. I think he could see there was no
point in keeping me with the kids.

I wasn't really back in the fold, though. One day there
was a reserve game at Carrow Road against Arsenal. And I

was playing centre back. I knew this was to wind me up. But, of course, being professional, I did what I was told and we battered them 4-1 with me giving a very accomplished display in my new position, if I do say so myself!

Andy Millen, my friend at St Mirren who I talked to so often during all that time, said, 'It will end. And when it does, you will be stronger because of it'. He also said, 'And one day the same thing will happen to another player and you can pass on your experience to him' — and that has happened, although at the time I was going through it I did find it difficult to see it that way.

Then, suddenly, there was another change. The manager had me back, travelling with the first-team squad to away games. I didn't get on the bench, but I was in the squad. And one day he singled me out in front of the group and said how well I'd been training and that I deserved to be with the group. It seemed like his way of announcing that I should be grateful to be allowed back. And perhaps, with results not going at all well, he had decided that I might be too good to be completely discounted. If he had picked me, I would have played. Of course I would. I was desperate to play for Norwich. But not for him.

Yet, in the January, he put me on the bench for an FA Cup game at Charlton. It was the first time since that defeat at Plymouth that I'd been on the first-team match-day team-sheet: 419 days.

Of the list of players that had been told to train with the kids all those months ago, I was the only one still there. Chrissy Martin and Michael Spillaine had gone to Luton on long loans and the rest had left. I believe the manager had tried to break me. But he sure as hell didn't succeed.

For the Charlton game, I roomed with Arturo Lupoli: a great guy. He said, 'If I score tomorrow, I am going to run to you'.

I said, 'Don't you dare. Do not come near me'.

Sure enough, he scored! So he came running towards the dugout looking for me. I was trying to make myself scarce though. I didn't want him to single me out and attract any attention. I just wanted to keep my head down and get on with things.

Arturo's goal earned us a 1-1 draw, but ten days later, in the replay at Carrow Road, Charlton, who were struggling like us in the League, beat us 1-0. The manager was dismissed the next day. Selfish or not, I remember thinking, 'the nightmare is over at last'.

Bryan Gunn was placed in charge. He told me, 'Right. You will get a chance to show me you should be in my team'. And Gunny brought Ian Crook in as a coach, who was like Andy Millen had been for me: full of encouragement and an unbelievable footballing brain.

In March, we were away to Birmingham. We had a team meeting on the day before the game and Gunny said, 'You have been waiting for your chance…' He turned the board over and I was in the team. Honestly, to this day, I get choked up thinking about that moment.

My dad came down to watch the game, and Jill was there, as usual. It was 16 months since my last Norwich first-team appearance and my family knew what that meant to me. Jill must have been keen to see the match as she ended up reversing down a motorway when she flew past the exit she was to take!

It was only a 1-1 draw (Cameron Jerome scored for them), and I wasn't brilliant but did fine. I played the full 90 minutes, in midfield, and afterwards I went over to the fans. They'd always been great to me and I think they sort of understood I had stayed about because I wanted to play for Norwich so much.

It was a personal victory to be back in the side, but there were nowhere near enough victories for the team. We lost at home to Sheffield Wednesday, and then we went to Swansea, the best footballing side in the division, and lost again. I was dropped to the bench and the lads beat Watford at Carrow Road, so I was still on the bench when we lost at Ipswich and then at home to Reading.

We had to win at Charlton on the last day of the season to have any chance of staying up. They were already relegated. I was recalled to the team but we lost 4-2 and the club was heading to the third tier. It was terrible. You looked at the stand behind the goal and it was packed with Norwich fans and we'd let them all down. And even though I'd not been involved for most of the season, I felt the guilt about being in the team that was going into the third tier.

On a personal level, I was out of contract, which was a worry. But Gunny held meetings with all the players to see who was prepared to stay. I told him that I definitely wanted to. He said he wanted me too.

That was the summer that Jill and I got married, which was a lovely distraction from the misery of what had happened to the club. But we were now thinking about our future as a married couple and I still had no formal offer from the club. So I was sitting in the Maldives on honeymoon thinking, 'I don't have a job!' There was no phone signal and no wifi, so I used to go to reception every day and borrow their computer to check for emails. But I believed Gunny would give me a contract, and when we got back to England, he did. I'll always be extremely grateful to him — he rescued my Norwich career twice: by bringing me back into the fold and then giving me a new deal when my contract ran out.

But the first game of the new season was the 7-1 defeat by Colchester at Carrow Road — and I wasn't quite so grateful to Gunny for asking me to go and warm up when we were 5-0 down! He must have double-checked my goal scoring record, though, as he decided to leave me on the bench!

That was another truly terrible day, and it was a shock to us all. Pre-season we had beaten everyone but, as I had seen before, it all counts for nothing come that first game. There was a sort of festival atmosphere before the game, as if everyone was sure we were too good for that division and 'only' playing Colchester. Well, Paul Lambert, who was the Colchester manager, used all that against us. And I remember someone saying that Michael Theoklitos, a lovely lad and our goalkeeper that day, had forgotten to put his thumbs on.

We had friends staying with us and had booked a nice meal out, so I had to sit there and keep my head down because I thought I probably shouldn't be showing my face in the city that night. Then, as planned, we went to a bar. Honestly, if I'd been able to find a balaclava I'd have put it on so that no fans would recognise me.

I went on as a sub in the next game, at Yeovil in the League Cup. We won 4-0 and we stayed down in the West Country because we were playing at Exeter on the Saturday. But on the Thursday, I think it was, we got called to a meeting and Gunny stood there and told us he'd been dismissed. You could see in his face how terrible it was for him.

Like with Peter Grant, I felt guilty when Gunny went. He had looked after me and I hadn't been able to repay him.

None of us could have guessed the impact our new manager, Paul Lambert, would have though. From the moment he first walked into our dressing room he had a manner about him that made you take notice. He asked a couple of players what they thought about the team and stuff, but then he said, 'I am going to give you my take on it,' which he duly did. He finished by saying 'we are going to win this division'. To some people it might have sounded crazy given our position but, and I think I can speak for everyone in that room, we were sat there believing him.

From his first match, he made every one of us know exactly what was expected of us. He didn't over-complicate things, though, and he always expected us to win the game. He had this unbelievable knack of making you feel 10 feet tall — he had such great belief in you. To have someone showing that belief in me so soon after a manager who'd had none meant the world to me.

I played 50 times that season. And for one game, in the Johnstone's Paint Trophy against Brentford, he made me captain. It was only for one match but for me, after what I'd been through at Norwich, to lead the side out at Carrow Road was brilliant and a real proud moment.

He got us so fit. And confidence was sky-high. We played with our chests out, Grant Holt led from the front, and you looked around the dressing room and you could see the belief and the determination. Everyone bought into everything the manager said and did. He had us in the palm of his hand. If he had told us to jump out of a window, we'd have been half way through it before he'd finished telling us. But he didn't rule by fear. We just respected what he'd done as a player and what he was doing with us.

At the turn of the year we won 1-0 at Wycombe to get in the top two. Then, two games later, we went to Colchester, determined to pay them back for what had happened in the first game of the season. We won 5-0, on a pitch that was so bad that I was covered from head to toe in mud and looked like I had just completed an army assault course or something. That was the first time I learned about the King of Spain business. I'd been hearing something with my name in it but not been able to work out what the fans were singing. But after that game at Colchester, Jill said, 'They're calling you the King of Spain!'

It was a bit surreal, but it was really great to have the fans singing a song about me. Years later, after I'd left the club,

I came back for the last home game of the 2012-13 season against West Brom, and myself and Ads were introduced on the pitch before the game. Although it had been a while, 26,000 supporters singing the King of Spain still made the hairs on the back of my neck stand up.

The Colchester game was in the middle of eight consecutive victories. Leeds were our only real rivals for the title, and when they came to Carrow Road in the March, Chrissy Martin scored the only goal of the game in the last minute. There was a great picture of him wheeling away with his fists clenched and his face roaring in triumph. Behind him there is a Leeds player, face down in the turf in despair, and hurdling over that guy there's me chasing after Chrissy with the biggest grin on my face as if I had just scored the goal.

We made sure of promotion four games before the end of the season — at Charlton, where we'd had that terrible day the year before. Then we beat Gillingham at Carrow Road to seal the title with two games to go. What an incredible feeling that was!

They gave us the trophy at the last game of the season, at our ground — where we'd had that 7-1 defeat. We actually lost to Carlisle that day but didn't care at all. At one point we'd been a massive 15 points behind Leeds, but now we were Champions, and we lifted the trophy in front of our fans. For me, personally, it vindicated my determination to stay. My wife and family had seen me at my lowest, so it must have been great for them to see the celebrations and know what I was feeling. I was euphoric.

For the next season, in the Championship, the manager brought in a new group of players — guys like Elliott Ward, Andrew Surman, David Fox, Andrew Crofts and John Ruddy and, just like the players who were already there, they all bought into his way of thinking. I don't think anyone outside the club expected us to go from League One, arrive in the Championship and nearly win that division as well. But the Gaffer said to us, 'We go again'. And we did.

It wasn't a coincidence that we kept getting goals right at the death. If we were losing at half-time, the Gaffer would still make us believe we were going to win. And it became sort of self-fulfilling. We thought we could, so we were charging forward. Opposition teams thought we could, so they fell back. The crowd thought we could and roared us on.

It felt that the whole club, the whole city and all of Norfolk were part of the same incredible mission. The numbers we took to away games were unbelievable. You'd go out onto the pitch and there would be this wall of yellow at one end making a hell of a noise.

I played another 30 games in the Championship season, despite missing a part of it with appendicitis. I was on the bench for the evening game at Portsmouth in May. Cardiff, our rivals for the second promotion place, were playing in the afternoon at home to Middlesbrough and expected to win. If they lost, though, and we won, we'd be promoted. The manager said, 'Don't concern yourselves with Cardiff, just concentrate on doing our job later'. As if that was ever going to happen!

I was sitting watching the Cardiff game in my hotel room with Stephen Hughes, and when Cardiff conceded an early goal, we were punching the air. When Cardiff conceded a second goal, we went out onto the corridor and every single Norwich player came out of his room and was in that corridor. But because the manager had told us not to bother about the Cardiff game, and because we were in a hotel, we were all sort of celebrating by mime — hugging each other and high-fiving more or less in silence. When Cardiff went 3-0 down and it was still the first half, some of the lads were running up the corridor with their tee-shirts over their heads and stuff like that but, again, not shouting out loud what we all felt.

On the bus to go to Fratton Park for our match, I sat there thinking, 'We are going to do this!' I remember Russ Martin and Andrew Crofts walking past me to their seats and we just stared at each other as if we were all thinking the exact same thing. It had felt like that for nearly two seasons in our dressing room. We would stand in the tunnel before games, look at the opposition and think, 'You know what? Whatever you do, we are going to have more than you — as individuals and as a group — and we are going to beat you'.

So at Portsmouth, I sat on the bench convinced that someone on our side would do something that would win the game. And I had the perfect view as it happened. Foxy looked up and hit a ball. I couldn't see who it was aimed at, but then I spotted Simeon Jackson running towards the far post and realised that Foxy had picked him out with an absolutely unbelievable pass. Of course, Jacko scored with a diving header.

I was sent on for the last four or five minutes, and that, among so many other things, is why Paul Lambert is another man I owe so much to. He kept me, played me, gave me another contract, and he put me on the pitch for the moment when Norwich won promotion to the Premier League. I only hope I repaid the faith he showed in me in his time at the club.

That summer our first child, Olivia, was born. It was a special, special time. But just before the pre-season I tore my calf whilst out running as part of my close-season programme. I missed the first week of pre-season and I knew I had a fight on my hands anyway. I hadn't always been a first pick in the Championship and now the manager would strengthen the squad. But I also knew it might be my only shot at the Premier League and wanted to stay. I had opportunities to go out on loan but the manager said he wanted me to stay and be part of it all. That was all the convincing I needed.

I played in the League Cup but didn't get a Premier League game until the January — when I was picked for the match at QPR. In the end I played four league games, and I treasured every minute of them. We won three of them and drew 3-3 at Arsenal. I was unbeaten in the Premier League!

The last of my four was the final game of the season, at home to Aston Villa. I played the full 90 and at the end, when the players walked around the pitch, I had Olivia with me and she was wearing her tiny Norwich scarf. I was so proud.

It had been wonderful being involved with Norwich in the top division, but I only had a finite number of seasons left as a player and I was thinking I would have to move on to be playing regularly again. But then, that summer, the manager left and went to Villa, and Chris Hughton came in. So I thought, 'I won't jump ship just yet because I don't know what my prospects might be'.

I played for Chris in the League Cup in August, against Scunthorpe, and managed to score my first goal for Norwich for more than five years — a good strike from just outside the box. But I picked up an injury in that game and was out until November, so when a chance came to go on loan to Cardiff I took it. I realised that meant my time at Norwich was more or less up.

I did, however, manage one more appearance that season — my last as a Norwich City player. I came back to Norwich briefly after the end of the Cardiff loan and played in a 3-0 win at Peterborough in the FA Cup.

A few weeks later my move to Cardiff became permanent. As I drove away from Colney for the last time, I was absolutely gutted. However, like any walk of life, football will inevitably throw you highs and lows, and when I look back on my six wonderful years at the club, the former most definitely outweigh the latter.

Later on I had a loan spell at Sheffield United, and later still I had two seasons with St Johnstone. We did move to Scotland but we always thought we'd end up back in Norfolk. Both our children — a little boy, Sam, came along in 2014 — were born at the N&N and most of the time my wife and I had spent together as a couple had been here. We wanted to bring our kids up in Norwich, and so now we have our home just outside the city.

Not, you might still be surprised to learn, anywhere near Spain.

Simon Lappin made 126 Norwich appearances between January 2007 and January 2013, and played for the club in three divisions. He was on the pitch when City were relegated to League One, but also when they were promoted to the Premier League two years later.

2

Any list of Norwich City greats has to include **Terry Allcock**. You can find a few grainy clips of his era on YouTube, but here is his full story — a truly epic Tale of a supremely gifted sportsman who played with and against some of the most famous names in football. And, along the way, he explains why his own sense of what was right prevented him from becoming the club's all-time leading scorer.

BREAKING BONES AND RECORDS

BY TERRY ALLCOCK

When the local media and supporters talk to me, they want to hear about Norwich City's 1959 FA Cup run — when we were in the old Third Division but got as far as a semi-final replay.

To be honest, it's not really among my personal highlights. When you score two goals in the first 20 minutes of your debut, as a 17-year-old, for one of the country's top teams, against one of the most famous goalkeepers ever, then you've done something that will stay with you all your life. So when people ask me about my career highlights, I don't have to think much further than the very start.

But the Cup run was something special to be involved in, and I understand why it meant so much to the club, the city and the county at the time, and it is certainly something I am proud to have taken part in — particularly because of how we played, which is something people get wrong.

When people read about it or hear about that great Cup run now, they imagine that we must have been fighters, scrapping our way through games. But we didn't kick anybody off the pitch. We played football and beat good sides with our quality.

I had joined Norwich from Bolton (for whom I'd made that debut as a teenager). I came to Norwich in March 1958, and the Cup run was the very next season — my first full campaign for the Canaries.

Our manager, Archie Macaulay, had assembled a good group: experienced players and guys from some of the biggest clubs in the country at that time. And we were probably one of the first-teams to play 4-4-2. The new system came about when the manager tried it out against Southend at Carrow Road in the League at the start of January. We won 4-0. Terry Bly and Errol Crossan scored one each and I scored two and obviously the manager was satisfied and so he kept the formation.

Our Cup run had started two months before that, though, because, as a Third Division Club, we had to play in the first round. We had a home tie against Ilford, a non-League team, who we beat 3-1. That didn't give anybody any hint at all of what was to come, and nor did the next round, when we took two games to finish off Swindon, who were in the same division as us.

But now we were into the third round, and who should come out of the hat but Manchester United.

There was an inch of snow on the Carrow Road pitch for the United game, but they just swept the lines clear and marked them blue. We played with a bright red ball. The police had put a restriction on the crowd of 38,000, but that was more than enough to create a tremendous atmosphere and we won 3-0. Terry Bly got two and Errol Crossan got the other. It was a really tremendous result against Matt Busby's famous 'Babes' and the *Pink Un* headline was, 'Bly, Bly Babes'.

Bly was the surprise of the whole business. The manager had got all these players in from big clubs, but Bly was a 22-year-old from a village in Norfolk who was one of our reserves. He just stepped in at the turn of the year because we were short. He was a big strong lad — a tremendous striker of a football — who had an outstanding period in the Cup. But the following season after the Cup run, he left for Peterborough.

Once we'd beaten Manchester United, we became a big news story nationally. And for the draw for the next round, on the Monday lunchtime, we were invited to the Mayor's parlour in City Hall, where we had a sherry reception and gathered around a radio to listen to the numbers being pulled out. And, for every round after that, we were invited to City Hall for the draw. It became a sort of ritual.

Unless you were around at the time, it is hard for you to understand the effect of us beating Manchester United. All the principal newspapers had people staying in Norwich to get stories. They were all at the Royal Hotel, which was at the top of Prince of Wales Road. The building is still there, across the road from Anglia TV. It's all offices now.

The journalists followed us about, trying to sneak into training sessions and the like, but they weren't the only people who descended upon Norwich. Some spivs came up from London and were selling black-market tickets down by the river, and the story was that some locals threw them in the water.

So there was all this activity and excitement in the city as we built up to the fourth round — at home to Cardiff. They were in the division above us and it was a tight game on a pitch that was difficult because it was a bit frozen again, but we managed to win 3-2. So it was back to the Mayor's parlour.

The draw for round five gave us Tottenham away and more than 20,000 City fans travelled to the capital by road and rail. The team went by rail and, from time to time, when we could spot the road, we would see all the cars and coaches with Norwich flags waving out of the windows.

The attendance was close to 75,000. We had a chance more or less from the kick-off, when young Bly turned in their area, but he couldn't quite dig the ball out from under his feet to get any power into the shot. They had a few chances but it was 0-0 at half-time, and we had a lot of pressure at the start of the second half. Then came my one FA Cup goal of the whole run. I hold all sorts of scoring records for Norwich but only scored once in the Cup that season because I was playing more of what today would be called a holding role. My goal against Spurs came when Matt Crowe slid in a very well weighted pass, just behind the centre-half, for me to run on to. As their goalkeeper, John Hollowbread, came rushing out towards me, I tucked the ball away quite easily with my left foot.

Of course, there was no kissing each other, or sliding along the floor, or elaborate celebrations. You just walked or jogged back to your own half and you might get a slap on the back from one or two of the team. The Norwich fans were up that end, and they were certainly excited, but I never got carried away when I scored, because it was just part of my job.

They really came at us after that, but it looked as if we would hold out, but then, in the very last minute, Cliff Jones, their Welsh international winger, popped up in our area and scored the equaliser. It was 1-1.

When our train got back to Thorpe Station there were probably 3,000 people waiting to welcome us. They were crowded onto the platform and we couldn't get through. The railway people had to put us on the luggage trolley and wheel us through the crowd.

I think everybody thought that the replay would be the end of the road for us though — apart from the players. We were optimistic and full of confidence. The team spirit was tremendously high. Sometimes a team just comes together and it all clicks, and that was us. We all had our individual jobs to do, but as a unit we were quite solid.

Of course, there was another 38,000 in the ground for the Tottenham replay and it was a very tense sort of game. They made three changes, including bringing Danny Blanchflower[1] back into the team. Most of the players we faced that night

---

1   Danny Blanchflower was a Northern Ireland international who was Footballer Of The Year twice. He spent a decade at Spurs, captaining them to four trophies in three seasons at the beginning of the 60s.

would be part of their League and FA Cup double winning side two years later. But that night we were in control and got the only goal of the game in the 63rd minute from young Bly — with a shot from about the penalty spot.

That was another big scalp, and the national attention we were getting, and the excitement in Norwich, all built up even more. But one of the things that helped us, I believe, was that the manager liked routine. And our trainer, Harry Toppin — who had coached in Holland — was very jovial and he could break down any tension with a joke. He was a wonderful guy. Years later, when I broke my leg the first time, he used to cycle with me and make me go up Kett's Hill in Norwich for rehabilitation. We didn't have all the medical equipment that footballers have nowadays, but there were guys like Harry, who knew what would work.

So, during our Cup run, we had the manager and the trainer keeping things relatively normal. But the manager was also a bit superstitious, and he kept doing some little different things that had worked, to his mind, in the Cup. For instance, before the United game, in our Friday meeting after the team had been announced, he had a tray of drinks brought in. We all thought, 'Oh! Lovely.' But the drinks were a mixture of sherry, raw eggs and cream, and tasted awful — but because we won the game, the same drinks became part of our pre-match ritual for the rest of the Cup run.

A lot of the players had superstitions, about what they wore on match-days, or the order they lined up to go out on to the pitch and things like that. Barry Butler had to be behind the captain, and another one had to be last out — that sort of thing. But I didn't have any superstitions really. I am a bit laid-back, I suppose.

In the last eight of the Cup there were six teams from the top division, Sheffield United from the second and us from the third — and we were drawn away to Sheffield United. I had a problem as we prepared for that one. My big toe had been stamped on. It blew up to about twice its normal size and I had to go around in a plimsoll with the toe area cut out and missed training all week. On the Friday it was still bad, and so the club took me up to the hospital and the surgeon there lanced my toe, making a hole through the nail. The blood came out like a fountain, because the pressure had been unbelievable. But once it was out, the pain was gone and they strapped me up and I knew I could play.

We travelled to Sheffield later that day. That was around the time that the first motorway, the M1, was opened. But there weren't many good roads in Norfolk and we couldn't have a long journey on the day of a game.

Between 15,000 and 20,000 Norwich fans made the journey to Sheffield to support us. It was a very difficult game for us. They scored very early on and then we had an injury to our goalkeeper, Ken Nethercott, in the second half. Willie Hamilton went racing through for the home team, Nethercott dived at his feet and stopped the goal — but dislocated his right collarbone. He wouldn't come out of goal, though, because there were no substitutes then. He wasn't going to go and play on the wing and put someone in goal who had never done it before, so he played with one hand for the last 30 minutes.

We had to try to protect him. We closed things down and played a much more restricted game than was usual for us, but of course we were losing, so we had breakaway attacks when we could.

After 75 minutes, Bobby Brennan, our left-winger, cut into the penalty area and rolled the ball past their goalkeeper and along the six-yard line. Two of their defenders had gone over towards the near post, and so when the ball went past them, there was an open goal. Crossan and me were both steaming in, but he got there before me — he was quicker than me! — and he was on his own in front of an empty goal. So we drew 1-1.

That meant another replay at Carrow Road under lights on the Wednesday night. Playing under floodlights was a relatively new thing and it created the best atmosphere you could have. Under lights, on a rainy night, with a big crowd — that's the ideal football scenario.

The crowds at Carrow Road were enormous compared to what they get now. There were seats in the main stand but on the other three sides it was just terraces and the fans stood. When something exciting happened, there would be a surge as fans strained to see and toppled forward, pushing the spectators in front, who pushed the ones in front, and so on. Everyone ended up going down four or five steps of terracing in a mass of people. As players, we were very much aware of these big surges of people.

The connection between the fans and the players was even more special in Norwich, I believe, because it was a relatively small city and a tight community, and between games we mixed with the supporters all the time.

As a team, we used to have lunch at the Royal Hotel and walk to the ground down Riverside and the fans would be walking to the ground at the same time. You just chatted to them and they chatted to us. I had a good relationship with the fans, who liked the way I played, and all of the players used to go to a lot of public events. We got so many invites, so we would go and play in darts tournaments and snooker tournaments, and judge beauty contests, and so on.

We were involved in articles in the press a lot, too. On one occasion we had a training session in Rhyl, Wales, prior to a game somewhere in the North West. I had a reputation for buying decent, quality clothes, and when we were sitting down to dinner, Crossan, who was our comedian stood up and called me 'The Count' and presented me with a cigarette holder. I didn't even smoke! The press got hold of my new nickname, and so a few days later they did a caricature in the paper of me wearing a cape, like something the aristocracy would wear on a night out.

Anyway, there was a tremendous atmosphere for the replay against Sheffield United and we scored after 13 minutes. Brennan showed the value of being two-footed. He was on the front edge side of their area, facing across the pitch with the ball on his right foot. So the fullback must have expected him to keep going across the front of the box, but he suddenly swerved to his left, completely beating the fullback, and then he hit a rising left-footed shot into the net, in front of the Barclay stand.

Bly got the second about a quarter of an hour later. He and a defender were racing for the ball, and their goalkeeper, Alan Hodgkinson, who was an England international, came out to try to get to it first. But Bly just got a touch to it to lob it over the goalkeeper.

Sandy Kennon had come into our side in goal because of the injury to Nethercott. He himself went on to be a very fine goalkeeper, but that night he sort of pushed one shot out to Derek Pace, who made it 2-1.

In the second half, Hodgkinson parried a shot to one of our players — Bly of course! So that made it 3-1 to us, and there was a little bit of a pitch invasion by some of our fans. Sheffield wouldn't lie down and Gerry Summers headed a second goal for them, but we kept creating chances too and deserved to win, I think. When the final whistle went, and it was 3-2 to us, the fans really did spill onto the pitch from all four sides. They came straight over the top of the walls around the pitch and carried us off shoulder high.

Three of the four sixth round games went to replays. So when the draw was made there were lots of 'either or' permutations. The winners of our replay were due to play the winners of a replay between Luton and Blackpool, and on the same night that we beat Sheffield, Luton beat Blackpool 1-0. The other semi-final ended up being Nottingham Forest v Aston Villa at Hillsborough.

Our game with Luton was to be at White Hart Lane — where we'd already secured a draw against Tottenham in round five — and, to be honest, we thought Luton would be easier opponents than some we had already had to deal with.

Luton were very physical. They made a beeline for both our wingers. They knew Crossan was very quick — if I knocked a poor ball down the line he was so quick he'd make it look a decent ball. Luton kicked lumps out of him that day. They took the lead in the first half, with a header by Allan Brown, but we got a second half-equaliser from our other winger, Brennan. He'd come in from the left and when the ball reached him in the area, he hit it first time with his right and we were level. But it was one of our poorer performances. I think we had got to a stage when we were beginning to get a bit anxious because we were getting so close to Wembley. I was all right, because I played in a couple of rounds for Bolton the previous season before I joined Norwich, and they went on to win the Cup, so I had that experience behind me. But you could feel anxiety in our team, and it led to us missing one or two chances that people would normally have put away.

We had yet another replay to contend with — at Birmingham the following Wednesday. There was only one goal. The build-up was a bit messy, with a couple of deflected passes, but eventually, the ball fell to Billy Bingham,[2] near our left-hand post, and he knocked it in.

2   Billy Bingham went on to manage Northern Ireland and Everton, among others.

You can imagine the mood in our dressing room afterwards. With replays, that was our eleventh FA Cup match of the season. We had kept going so long and had got so close to the Final, but we'd just not managed it. We travelled back to Norfolk by a train that was full of our supporters. We drank the train dry by the time we got to Peterborough, and so the train was kept by the platform in Peterborough while they loaded more alcohol on. Ron Ashman, our captain, said, 'These supporters have been with us all the way on this Cup run, so let's walk through the train and, instead of them singing "On The Ball" to us, let's sing to them.' So we walked from front to back of the train and back a couple of times, singing 'On The Ball' and having a drink with supporters. Good days.

It would have been nice to have played at Wembley. It would have been interesting to see how we would have handled it. Later I went as a coach with Manchester City, but it's not the same and it would have been special to go there as a player with Norwich, from the Third Division.

At the end of the season, because we'd missed fixtures because of the Cup run, we played 11 League games in 25 days. That included one period of four games in seven days and one of three in five. Twice we played on consecutive days. And they say that footballers these days play too many games! We finished third, and so missed out on promotion — but we got it the following year.

Three years after our famous FA Cup run, Norwich won the League Cup. It was only in its second season and hadn't become as big as it did once they moved the final to Wembley, but it was still something to win it — but I broke my leg at Halifax in the semi-final.

I look back now and think that the 59 Cup run was a tremendous time, and I am grateful to have been part of it. But, as I say, I had other highlights in my career and I played with or against everyone who was anybody. You don't realise until you've finished the quality of the players you've come up against. In my second game, I had to mark Len Shackleton,[3] I was in matches with John Charles,[4] Bobby Moore,[5] Tom Finney,[6] Stanley Matthews,[7] Georgie Best,[8] Denis Law,[9] and people of that calibre.

I was very, very fortunate. I was just one of those people blessed with a natural ability with a football — and not only a football: a ball of any shape and size. I was in my school under-15 football team in Leeds when I was eight. By the time I was 12 I was captain of Leeds boys, and by the time I was 13 I was captain of Yorkshire boys. I played for the North of England and I played for England boys against The Rest with Duncan Edwards and David Pegg. They went on to play for Manchester United and England, but were both killed in the Munich air disaster. A lot of good judges think Duncan was the best player England ever had, although he was only 21 when he died. David was just 22. When we played for England boys together, they were my room-mates.

At the same time, I captained Leeds boys at cricket. I was opening batsman and wicket-keeper, and on my first appearance, I scored 87. My next game was for Yorkshire boys and I opened the batting and top scored with 65 (against Derbyshire).

3   Len Shackleton, the 'Clown Prince of Football', scored 134 goals in just over 11 seasons with Newcastle and Sunderland.

4   John Charles, the 'Gentle Giant', played for Leeds, Juventus, Roma and Cardiff.

5   Bobby Moore, England's World Cup winning captain.

6   Sir Tom Finney, won 76 England caps and made 569 appearances for Preston.

7   Sir Stanley Matthews, the 'Wizard of the Dribble', knighted while still playing. First European Footballer of the Year

8   George Best, 'El Beatle', scored as Man Utd won European Cup for the first time. Regarded as best British player of all time.

9   Denis Law went to Torino for a then record £110,000, then to Man Utd, where he is behind only Wayne Rooney and Bobby Charlton in the scoring list.

My school became a primary school so I had to be transferred to another school, which was a Rugby League school, and I ended up playing Rugby League for the county. But then, and I am sure it was through the football authorities, I was moved to the best football school in Leeds.

After I left school I earned money from both football and cricket. When I was playing football with Bolton I was still registered for Yorkshire for cricket and they wouldn't release my contract. Well, I couldn't travel to Yorkshire to play, so I played Lancashire League cricket. I played against all the top players in the world. I played against Sonny Ramadhin and Alf Valentine in 1959 — the year that they took 59 wickets between them for the West Indies in a Test Series in England. I made 80-odd not out against them.

At football, I was straight into Bolton reserves at 15 and made my first-team debut at 17 at Manchester City, seven miles up the road from Bolton. Bert Trautman[10] was their goalkeeper and my direct opponent was Don Revie.[11]

There were about 60,000 spectators and I scored two goals in the first 20 minutes. I can still remember them because your first game always stays in your memory. The first goal came when a good ball was slipped into the area for me, I took one touch and then, bang, it was in — a left-footed shot. The second was quite similar but it was with my right foot.

I was a natural scorer. The best strikers don't stop the ball. If you stop it, to control it or get it into a better position, the defender will make up two yards or the goalkeeper will adjust his feet and be ready, and you will have lost the opportunity. You have got to take the shot on your first touch. And you have

---

10   Bert Trautman, a German paratrooper, was a prisoner of war. He played on with a broken neck in the 1956 FA Cup Final.

11   Don Revie, innovative player, went on to manage Leeds United, whom he made a major force, and England.

got to have a policy that, if someone is shooting from the right, you follow in from the left or vice versa. You might make ten runs but it will come to you once — the goalkeeper will knock it down to you or the shot will come across to you. You've just got to keep making the runs.

At Bolton I deputised for Nat Lofthouse[12] at centre-forward sometimes, but my true position was inside-forward and it didn't matter if it was inside-left or inside-right. Most of the pictures of me playing show me jumping for a header or firing a shot, and make me look like a big, bustling sort of player. But, as an inside forward, I had to be skilful. I wasn't particularly quick but I had a very good engine, and I didn't really know which was my favourite foot because I was equally adequate on either side. And I could head a ball. In those days, as an inside-forward, you were expected to be defending one minute and scoring the next. If you didn't get 15 goals a season, you thought you were a flop.

Anyway, in 1958, when I was 22, I went into work one Monday morning and the manager said they'd had an offer from Norwich. I said, 'Where the hell is that?'

So why did I go to Norwich, which meant stepping down two divisions? Well the wages were capped no matter what division you were in, and the environment was certainly an improvement. I'd been brought up in Leeds, which was an urban jungle, and I'd lived in Bolton, which was the same, so before I came to Norwich I had never ever seen trees in a street. I was married by the time I came to Norwich and our eldest son was 18 months, so to move somewhere where you didn't have to go to a park to see a tree was a big thing. My wife was a Blackpool girl, so she liked the fact that we could get to the coast quite easily.

---

12   Nat Lofthouse, 'The Lion Of Vienna', England's centre-forward, scored 255 goals in 452 Bolton appearances.

I signed for Norwich in March 1958, just before the transfer deadline, and I immediately got the offer of a job coaching cricket at Gresham's School, in Holt, that summer. They paid me travel expenses and a good salary, on top of my football wages, so we were more than happy to be at Norwich.

I see all the great players now because I host the match-sponsors at Carrow Road every game. But I am often bored by the way the game is played. The build-ups can be so slow and methodical. I think that is the influence of all the continental players who are over here. They have learned to play that way because of the climate and conditions with which they grew up. When we played, we were playing in four inches of mud, covered in sand to soak it up, with a ball that was like a piece of lead. So you couldn't stroke three or four sideways passes. Now they play four or five and it goes back to the goalkeeper!

It was a different game. In my day it was very physical. You had to kill somebody to get sent off, and I broke both legs, broke my nose four times, broke my collarbone and had five metatarsal injections. Rooney and Beckham had five months off when they broke their metatarsals. We used to go to the hospital at noon for a pain-killing injection and then just go and play in the afternoon.

When I had my second leg break in the League Cup semi-final at Halifax, the trainer came on and did what they always did in those days — rub the injury with the 'magic' sponge from a bucket of cold water. I played on for 75 minutes and only found out afterwards that my leg was broken.

I take satisfaction from being the second highest all-time goal-scorer for Norwich, with 127 in 389 games, although at the end of my career, after I had broken my legs, I played more games at centre-back than anywhere else. For five seasons I didn't score a goal. While I was off with the second broken leg, Norwich bought Ron Davies, an excellent centre-forward, and so I played as one of two centre-backs. I was in the Bobby Moore role, tidying up alongside the other centre-back. I enjoyed it, but I never went up for corners. If I had, I would probably have got at least the five more goals that would have made me level as all-time top Norwich scorer with Johnny Gavin. But when I was a forward I used to hate defenders coming up for corners and getting in my way. I used to leave a space to run into, but then a big defender from my own team would come and take the space I had created, so when I was a centre-back I didn't use to do it.

But I still hold the record for 37 goals in a season. That was in the 1962-63 season, when there was a really hard winter and a long time when nobody in the country could play any games. We had 14 weeks without matches, but we hired a hangar at Norwich Airport and used to play full practice games on the concrete floor in plimsolls. Norwich were in the second tier, and didn't have a particularly good season. They finished mid-table, yet that was when I got my 37 goals.

I am the only Norwich player to have scored a hat-trick in the League, the FA Cup and League Cup in the same season. I scored five hat-tricks in total for Norwich, which is another record. I scored seven goals in one week: one against Stoke on the Saturday, four against Newcastle on the Wednesday, and two against Manchester City on the Saturday.

Alongside my playing, I started coaching. In the week I scored seven goals, I took my FA coaching practical exam at Keswick College in South Norfolk during the morning before playing against Newcastle at Carrow Road in the afternoon. The Wolves manager, Bill McGarry, was doing the assessing at the college and then came to the game and saw me score four goals — so he probably gave me a good mark for my practical!

I got a UEFA coaching licence (as well as an MCC cricket coaching qualification) and then began running coaching courses in Norfolk. Lol Morgan, the Norwich manager, was doing courses around the county too, and he got upset that the FA rang me to do the assessing of the people he had been teaching to coach. That didn't go down well. We had a bit of a falling out about that.

I had five managers at Norwich and Lol was the last one. It got to the Easter time and I knew I was coming to the end of my career. I played in the reserves at Swindon on the Friday. I went into the ground on the Sunday because I had blisters from playing on the hard ground and was having some treatment. The first-team had only won once in seven games. Lol saw me and said he wanted me to play the next day, Easter Monday, at home to Huddersfield – and he wanted me to play at centre-forward. I scored the only goal of the game and he got the sack. I hadn't played centre-forward for five years but I imagine there was so much pressure put on him by the board to pick me, and then, when he did, I scored. That sort of showed he'd been wrong to leave me out.

They interviewed me for the manager's job, but I didn't want it, so they told me they would like me to be coach and youth team manager. They gave me that job before they appointed anyone to be in charge of the first-team, and then they brought in Ron Saunders to be manager. He was infamous for making the players run up the hills on Mousehold Heath. Well, I was the guy at the top of the hill sending them down again!

Ron and I got along famously. And when he was sacked, he got offered the job at Manchester City and I resigned from Norwich to go with him. That was 1973. I'd been at Norwich for 15 years.

Ron and I were at Manchester City the season we relegated Manchester United — a famous occasion when Denis Law back-heeled the winner for City but refused to celebrate because of what the goal did to his former club, United.

I bought a house in Manchester but we never moved up there. We had five children in education in Norfolk, and I came back to Norwich after games every weekend. When Ron fell out with the Manchester City chairman, Peter Swales, I decided I wouldn't go to Aston Villa with him. I didn't want to live in the Midlands and I wasn't really enthusiastic about coaching. It wasn't as good as playing and I wanted to be with my family. So I moved back, although I had never really left.

Terry Allcock scored 127 goals in 389 Norwich appearances, despite moving back to the defence for the end of his City career. He went on to coach the team as they won promotion to the top division for the first time.

3

Tim MacWilliam moved to Norfolk so he could watch Norwich regularly. Now he provides commentaries of their matches for visually impaired supporters. Yet he has a guilty secret. He used to support a team who play in blue (no, not that one). But, after years of divided loyalty, another broadcaster's insults made him realise his true love. This is his application for Canary citizenship.

MISSING KEN, FINDING MY CLUB

BY TIM MACWILLIAM

It's not unknown for the Norwich City faithful to describe their loyalty in terms of bleeding yellow and green. However, although I might even include myself among them, my blood is likely to have a strange tint as it once ran blue and white!

For many, changing or even sharing your football loyalty is a sin, and at times it still makes me cringe. Perhaps I'll never be considered a pure yellow, or completely erase memories from that previous liaison.

My family actually has form for this. My grandfather was club doctor at Brentford, and everyone supported the Bees. However, I grew up in Berkshire and followed nearby Reading. Eventually, my mum changed her allegiance to the Royals too and, given that she was jokingly referred to as 'a bit of a turncoat' at her funeral, she clearly was never completely forgiven.

Similarly, some will never accept me as a 'proper' Norwich fan. I had that confirmed one Saturday lunchtime at Future Radio, the city's community station, which is run by a charity. I'm one of the volunteer presenters, but on this particular day two of us had been booked by mistake to front the sports show. Neither of us backed down and the uneasy truce of co-presenting soon descended into an ill-tempered bicker about whether some Norwich fans were actually justified in hoping for a defeat that would finally lead to the axe falling on Nigel Worthington. I suggested this was a disgrace and anyone thinking so was not a real fan. That was when the savage low blow was delivered.

'What do you care? You're not even a proper fan; you're a Reading supporter! You know you are!'

Several seconds of dead air ensued as I climbed off the canvas while considering a reply that wouldn't shut down the transmitter. The retort, when it came, was pretty feeble.

'I saw my first game at Carrow Road before you were born!'

Irrelevant and hardly a winning argument, but, nevertheless true. And some of you unforgiving readers might like to consider how long I've been afflicted with a passion for 'our' club. I first saw Norwich play in 1974 while on a family holiday in West Runton, having begged my parents to interrupt the holiday and make the trip to Carrow Road for the first game of the season. I even acquired a full Norwich City kit.

Stopping for petrol, we were served by a man who was so insistent that it was Bournemouth, and not the Canaries, playing that day, that we actually began to doubt it ourselves. The attendant realised his dry Norfolk wit and deadpan delivery were far too much for his rather dim customers and explained that John Bond had arrived the previous season, along with half the team from Dean Court.

We took a wrong turn, but picked up a hitchhiker clad in a yellow and green tank top who said he would navigate us to the ground in time for kick off. En-route he pointed out important historical monuments such as Kevin Keelan's old house and the spot where cars were pushed into the Wensum during a mini riot after relegation the previous season.

After we parked well away from any water, our hitchhiker, who appeared very well informed on all club matters, escorted us to the turnstiles. He recommended we view the match from the South Stand. Without warning, he became animated, pointing to a man who had just strolled past. 'That's Ken

Brown. Ken! Ken! All right Ken?' But, by the time I had worked out which direction to look, the man had disappeared through a door into the stadium. Our hitchhiker explained that the man I hadn't seen was the assistant manager and another import from Bournemouth. 'Really nice bloke, usually says hello', our hitchhiker-guide to the Norwich universe said, before explaining that Ken was probably too busy on a match day to stop and chat.

City were 2-0 ahead and coasting before Blackpool got one back and made it a nervous final few minutes (I didn't know I would need to get used to that). Norwich continued their great early season form until mid-September when they lost heavily at Craven Cottage (I had to get used to that too). I had a new football team in my life and the kit didn't come off until the start of the new school term.

I suggested we moved to Norfolk. After all, it seemed the ideal place to live: lots of nice beaches and we could watch Norwich City play every other week! But in the world of grown-ups, it wasn't practical, seemingly. 'You can come and live here when you are older' was the only straw of comfort offered by my mother. So we headed back to the M4 corridor and fourth tier football.

I watched the Norwich season from afar as it delivered promotion, and a League Cup final when only Kevin Keelan showed up at Wembley. The goalkeeper looked up from his penalty save and was aghast to witness his defenders carrying out an early day mannequin challenge as Ray Graydon smashed in the rebound.

Although I lived 160 miles from Carrow Road, I did get a chance to see Norwich once more. In 1980 they signed a player, Phil Alexander, from Wokingham Town and agreed to play a friendly as part of the deal. Wokingham played in the old Isthmian League on a tiny ground not far from my home. Over a thousand people crammed onto terraces made from old wooden railway sleepers to witness a surprisingly competitive match with a strong Norwich side, in which John Deehan equalised from a penalty late on.

Phil Alexander's playing career for the Canaries lasted a total of only 19 minutes. He later played American Football for the London Monarchs and later still became chief executive of Crystal Palace, but he made a young would-be Norwich fan very happy at the start of his short Carrow Road stay by making that friendly necessary. I recall that the players were dressed smartly, and were polite and courteous to anyone wanting a chat or an autograph. I hoped to meet Ken Brown, who had been promoted to manager by then, but he decided not to travel.

But I did see him five years later, in March 1985.

A PE teacher had given the devastating news I was never going to be a professional footballer and I was lurching from one dead end job to another. I went for an interview at a large four-star hotel in Beaconsfield. They had advertised for a live-in barman to start as soon as possible. On arrival it was noticeable something special was going on. The hotel had been decorated in yellow and green, including coloured napkins carefully folded into wine glasses. It was all in honour of one of the teams competing in that weekend's Milk Cup final.

Waiting in reception for my job interview, I saw across the lobby the BBC reporter Tony Gubba, who was conducting a different type of interview. He was filming with the players: Chris Woods, Asa Hartford and a permanently grinning Mick Channon. Each went through his short piece to camera, and then it was the turn of Ken Brown who was totally relaxed, as ever.

I temporarily abandoned my hotel application form and gawped at this sideshow. Ken smiled and winked. Suddenly embarrassed and not having a clue how to react, I returned my attention to the application form. 'Question five: What qualifications do you have?'

Not very many. But I wondered if the TV cameras might catch me in the background for an appearance in the package Gubba was putting together for *Football Focus*.

Ken Brown stayed in the lobby, with a drink in hand, as the BBC completed their work. I'm not sure if I imagined Ken would come over for a chat and just maybe bring a cup final ticket, but at that moment I was called for my own interview. I seriously considered throwing the job so I could discuss that imagined ticket with Ken. I probably should have.

I got the job. They wanted an immediate start and I could live in the staff quarters. I was taken to a tiny bedroom with no windows, akin to a cell. That night a fellow employee broke into the room to see if I had anything worth stealing. Fight or flight? I pretended to be asleep. When he left I stuffed everything that hadn't been nicked into my bag and headed out of my room and past the now silent lobby. Outside, the huge team coach was ready and waiting for daylight and the short trip to Wembley, while I made the journey back to my long-suffering parents.

In 1985, having the match on a Sunday was still a little uncommon and it was suggested there might be less passion from the fans. Ken had pointed out to a reporter that it would actually be Passion Sunday (the fifth Sunday of Lent) although this went over the journalist's head. Reporters do seem to ask some stupid questions.

I watched *Football Focus* and saw Tony Gubba's Norwich interviews, and I wasn't in any of the footage. So I had to wait three decades to feature, briefly, in a televised football item about Norwich. As I left Portman Road following the play-off semi-final in 2015, my phone was alarmingly full of messages, each one featuring a grainy screenshot taken from the Sky Sports coverage, accompanied with a barbed comment or insult. I was still receiving them several weeks later. I was the ugly fan wildly celebrating in super HD slow-motion when Jonny Howson's volley hit the net.

Ken Brown's Norwich won the Milk Cup, but my 1985 life was still devoid of any real direction. I was going nowhere.

Then two things happened. First, the hotel caught fire and half of it burned down — a terrible thing, but one which gave a bit of purpose to work: helping the hotel recover and re-open. The second significant event was that I managed to persuade the new head waitress to go on a date. Later I persuaded her to marry me and move to Norfolk.

Soon after we moved into our new home, November 9, 1987, the headline item on *Look East* was a tearful Ken Brown saying goodbye to his staff and well-wishers after being sacked by Norwich City. 'Such a lovely man,' said the women. 'Lovely bloke,' said the men. They all agreed this was not the way Norwich City did things. However, it was the way Robert Chase did things.

At this point, I was supporting two teams. But Reading were back in the fourth tier having done their own bit of yo-yo-ing and City, riding high in the top tier, would have been in Europe had it not been for UEFA ban on English clubs. So there was no conflict of interest and no problem for me. After all, Nick Hornby, famed Arsenal fan and author of *Fever Pitch*, devotes a whole chapter to his love of Cambridge United, and I happen to know a very senior journalist at the *Eastern Daily Press* has a passion for Burton Albion.

But three years after my move to Norwich, Reading got a huge injection of cash from John (later Sir John) Madejski. He had made money with the idea of placing photos next to classified car adverts and had used quite a lot of that money to save his local football club from extinction. With his cash, Reading moved up the leagues and, in 1998, moved away from the crumbling Elm Park ground into a bright new plastic stadium built on an old sewage dump. They also altered their badge.

The changes made my swing in loyalty slightly less emotionally challenging, because the club in Berkshire became somewhat removed from the one I had known.

The last match at Elm Park just happened to be against Norwich. So I went back and stood on the same terrace I knew so well from my boyhood, but this time with 3000 Norwich fans. Craig Bellamy rubbed salt into the wounds of the already relegated Royals by scoring a late winner. I celebrated the goal somewhat awkwardly and imagined the 8000 home fans were all looking at me accusingly.

While living in Bracknell I had begun to file football reports of Wokingham Town matches for local radio. I often travelled on the team bus to away games and the 'banter' from players was relentless and merciless, sometimes cruel and often silly. The useful advice on my first excursion was, 'Stay at the front of the bus and stare ahead.'

One player put on a Halloween mask and spooked the coach driver to the extent that he weaved all over the motorway, narrowly avoiding the central reservation. This didn't bother anyone else on board; they were mostly rolling around the bus as if it was a scene from *Gremlins*. The former Reading centre-forward Terry Bell bought joke soap that turned faces black in the post-match showers, and there was also a plastic rat which made customers scatter in service stations wherever we stopped.

So I was wary when, in the late eighties, I volunteered to work behind the bar at a Norfolk hotel for the Norwich City Christmas party. Would the players indulge in practical jokes in a similar vein to their non-League counterparts? Yes, they would.

Giggling City footballers carried out one prank after another: ice down backs, soda-syphon fights, and vigorously shaken bottles of champagne exploding as unsuspecting wine waiters opened them. I hid the fire extinguishers and made sure the swimming pool was locked, just in case.

Just before the bar closed, a pint of lager was purchased. I was instructed to tip most of it down the sink. The player, and I'll protect his modesty here, then left for the Gents and returned with the glass completely re-filled with a liquid of a similar colour. Grinning, he gave the spiked pint to his teammate, who took a gulp and, guess what? It wasn't funny!

I had anticipated things getting out of hand but hadn't expected to be holding back one of the players while others ushered away the prankster. The evening left a bad taste in the mouth in more ways than one.

By now my mother had become alarmed at my impending defection. 'Don't forget your roots', she implored, presumably regretting the purchase of that Norwich City kit many years ago. I was presented with a framed picture of the Madejski Stadium, just before we went there to see our teams play.

This was at the time when things were going sour for Nigel Worthington. We witnessed, at very close quarters, Dean Ashton knocked unconscious with the most sickening thud. He spent the rest of the match lurching around like a boxer who didn't know where he was or what he was doing. But no towel was thrown in by the Norwich bench. In stoppage time Ashton had the chance to equalise but took one of the worst penalties you will ever see. Even Rob Green would have saved it. To be fair, Ashton was probably looking at three or four balls and wasn't sure which one to kick.

After the game Worthy snapped angrily at the media and I sulked about the result. I think I was forgetting my roots.

My thoughts are often with the media following a poor defeat. Questions need to be asked and they will either be criticised for being too hard or too soft. It's a little like throwing in a verbal grenade, wondering if this one will detonate. Tin hats at the ready!

When Future Radio first went on air, Joe Ferrari, Norwich City's Head of Media, kindly allowed access to the pre-match interviews, known as Pressers (short for press conferences). These normally took place on a Thursday morning at Colney and I was surprised to learn the radio interviews were carried out in Worthy's own office, with cups of tea all round.

There was, though, a hierarchy to be observed. Radio Norfolk had first dibs, and then commercial radio offered a different perspective. Their reporter — and I haven't made this up — asked questions that would apparently be of interest to their core listener, visualised as a 25-year-old called Debbie. If any nationals were present they would go next, and then it was my turn, and I couldn't ask any questions that had gone before.

On my first attendance, Worthy greeted me with a jokey, verbal jab to the stomach: 'I won't stand for any stupid questions.'

The others all finished their interrogation on formation, dropped players, tactics, loan players, and the previous week's referee. I can't remember what questions were asked on behalf of Debbie as I was too busy working out what scraps were left for me.

No stupid questions. I had been warned. Perhaps I should ask about Passion Sunday.

'Are there any extra fitness issues with Youssef Safri while he observes Ramadan?'

The silence seemed to last for some time as I temporarily stopped breathing and braced myself for the onslaught of ridicule.

'Ah, Good question, you see!' Worthy said as he glanced at the others. They were waiting to go, but now, instead, turned their recording devices back on for the answer.

After Worthy had finished with me, I spotted Leon McKenzie in the distance and, buoyed by my success and unaware or forgetful of the etiquette of these occasions, I hurried over for a chat. Leon was very open, direct and honest on how he had been affected by some particularly spiteful rumours. We were promptly joined by other reporters, carrying cameras and big fluffy microphones, wanting a piece of this unexpected scoop.

At this point, Leon hurriedly departed and I received my first death-stare from a club official.

It was a long while before I was invited back to Colney again, by which time Glenn Roeder kept the press outside in the rain.

After being evicted from the press box on grounds that a proper journalist required my seat, I was asked by the club to get involved with Soccer Sight. It is a marvellous service providing match day description to visually impaired supporters, accessed via a headset anywhere in the ground. It is available for anyone, including the away fans and any others who would like some explanation of proceedings.

Given the service can reach all parts of the stadium it's remarkable the kit can be carried in a couple of large coat pockets. This is probably just as well as our commentary position is a moveable feast. Space permitting, we normally base ourselves near to wheelchair fans and their friends on the concrete gantry of the Ability Counts Stand.

Football on the radio was my constant escape while completing school homework, although I'm not sure I can blame those great commentators, Bryon Butler and Peter Jones, on a crackly medium wave radio for my concentration drifting from the American civil war to the latest England match. Sports commentary well done is almost poetic. So when I was invited onto a programme to share favourite music tracks, I chose audio archives of a non-musical variety instead. We heard Brian Moore from 1966: 'I thought that hit the bar and went in, Maurice Eddleston!' Obviously, there was room for a Canaries classic: 'Lansbury's corner… goes all the way through. Chance! Blocked on the line! It's going to go in!! You absolute beauty!!!'

I know Chris Goreham claims to be embarrassed by that shouted commentary to Simeon Jackson's dramatic winner against Derby as Norwich edged nearer promotion to the Premier League in 2011, but it is, indeed, an absolute beauty and if there is better local coverage or commentary than Radio Norfolk produce, I haven't heard it.

So why don't Soccer Sight listeners just take a pocket radio with them? One reason might be that our service is a little different, with description focused totally on the match and no reference to which horse is currently fourth in the Grand National, or the latest score from Wroxham. We have no digressions. We only talk about the match and we keep talking about the match. It helps those who are there, but who can't see very well, to make more sense of what they can see.

While attending a commentary course at Loftus Road, we were given an England match to describe on a giant plasma screen. Our tutor repeatedly screamed every time we forgot to inform our listener even for a split second. 'What's happening? Where's the ball? Tell me!'

A few days after the training, I received a call asking me if I would consider commentating for the partially sighted at the 2012 Olympic Games. I ran around celebrating like I had won gold. Months later, however, I received a less welcome message. The service had been cancelled due to a cut in funding, and my services would no longer be required.

I once asked Chris Goreham for some advice. 'Say what you see,' was the reply. Sounds easy, doesn't it? However, it would be most helpful if the away teams had clear numbers that don't merge into their shirts like some kind of chameleon font. There was some relief among our commentary team when Carrow Road's rotating screen was first installed but it's just out of focus from our viewpoint and yet another advert can replace the action at any given moment.

Listeners' comments are mostly positive but often mirror the performance on the pitch. I thought my first-half efforts in one of the relegation scraps had been fairly concise until a steely-eyed woman wearing a black, furry hat approached and clearly thought otherwise. 'Do you want some feedback?' Not quite so concise after all then.

When you spot a fan reacting to the action being described, it's a relief and also quite humbling. Occasionally I have found some of my match interpretations apparently being repeated on social media. Did I really say that about the referee?

I've watched games at Carrow Road from just about every part of the ground. However, I wouldn't want to have any other vantage point than the Ability Counts stand. Fans, stewards and commentators greet each other with hugs on match days and it's almost like a family reunion every match. Soccer Sight's David Newton is there first, setting up the kit, and he keeps us on air for the 90 minutes.

To commentate to these fans is an absolute joy, other than when I am forced to utter the words, 'Ipswich have scored.' Thankfully, those occasions are rare.

I try not to be too partisan, especially when we have away fans tuned in, although sometimes the fan in me takes over and things slip out that I later regret. I once turned the microphone off for a few seconds to give the referee some much needed advice, and I really shouldn't have referred to Middlesborough as cheats that night in 2015 when they ended the Canaries' chances of automatic promotion.

One game against Villa was so dull and boring, with both sides intent on a goal-less draw, that I noticed a listener nearby who was losing interest. So I thought I would try a different approach and let out a mini rant. 'What a terrible game; nothing has happened. Neither side has had a single shot. It's the worst game of the season!' At half-time I heard nearby mutterings. 'Who does he think he is? Alan Green?'

The most challenging moments are when I just haven't a clue what is going on. During the short tenure of Neil Adams, Leeds United arrived at Carrow Road for a mid-week match. In the first half, for no apparent reason, referee Mark Clattenburg stopped the game and the delay went on for several minutes. No one was injured but there was some arguing and a huddle and animated discussion by the dugout. I started to hypothesise about the reason for the stoppage, but could not come up with one for the lengthy stoppage in play. That was terrible, because I wanted to explain to the listeners, but couldn't explain it to myself. And what made it worse at the time was that I assumed the guys from BBC and Sky were right across it and knew exactly what is happening.

Except, they didn't. I found out later that nobody knew what was going on. It emerged after the game that Cameron Jerome claimed he had suffered racist abuse from an opponent.

Then there was the time when, instead of providing the Soccer Sight commentary, I had to rely on it to know what was going on — at one of the biggest matches in Canaries' history.

We were about to commentate on the second leg of the 2015 play-off semi-final against Ipswich. The atmosphere crackled while we discussed our view that it might go to extra-time and then a penalty shoot-out. Would we be describing John Ruddy saving the vital spot-kick from Daryl Murphy?

I was on first-half duty, but five minutes in a migraine descended and my own vision was impaired by flashing spots and zigzags. I squinted through and carried on the best I could. I made it to half-time and it was with some relief that I passed the baton, as it were, to my co-commentator, Toby Newton.

Early in the second half, I could tell through the continuing haze that something exciting and very positive for Norwich had happened, although I wasn't sure what. A full explanation came from Toby through my headphones. 'Penalty to Norwich and Ipswich are down to ten men!'

And I thought, 'This commentary service is pretty good!'

After the match, as my migraine subsided, my youngest daughter, Vicky, found something interesting. She is another member of our commentary team, albeit one who can't quite trust herself to commentate on Ipswich matches. She found a document flapping around near the Norwich dugout. It contained a series of pictures, seemingly produced by the City goalkeeping coach, showing the Ipswich penalties history for the season and where spot-kicks were likely to be put in the event of a shoot-out. So Ruddy might well have been able to make that save we'd imagined.

Oddly it was a commentator who unwittingly helped me complete the total transfer of my football allegiance on a traumatic evening when Norwich were all but relegated — April 27, 2009.

It was the final home game, Norwich were already practically doomed to relegation to the third tier and just guess who they were playing? Yep, Reading. However, it wasn't just what happened on the pitch that night which finally completed my 'transfer'.

I started the evening with at least a backwards glance to the visitors' promotion prospects, even if I didn't want to admit it. But my principal concerns were with Norwich, whose dismal home campaign I had watched unfold from the press box in a seat two rows from the back, directly in front of the away local radio commentary team. During that grim 2008-09 campaign, the visiting local radio commentators were often fans with microphones. Most went home happy as City slipped further into the mire.

The guys from commercial radio were the loudest and would scream their pre-recorded reports down the line, ending with the obligatory plug for an energy drink. 'Why didn't you do it live?' I asked. 'We can't afford mistakes. The advertisers don't like it', came the reply.

City's relegation to league one was still avoidable, just, but in reality, that final home game of the 2008-09 season at Carrow Road was going to be tough as Reading were still in the hunt for promotion.

City fans often talk about a crunch game as 'a potential Burnley', in reference to that torrid afternoon in front of live cameras where City lost 4-1, Garry Doc was sent off and the toxic atmosphere turned up to the maximum as Andy Hughes tried to Cantona a home fan. That evening, Nigel Worthington finally lost his job. The hero of Cardiff and that magical title-winning season was shown the door. Perhaps every manager has his use-by date, whatever his achievements.

That Monday night in April 2009 wasn't quite like that, because Bryan Gunn had only taken over as manager in the January, and few fans had turned on him, but the atmosphere was certainly full of dread and despair — except for the area where away fans were full of the fear that comes with hope. Reading could go up if they won their last two fixtures of the season.

I was in my seat early, heart pounding. I knew of the away commentator, who was well regarded and a big fan of the visitors. And when the away radio station went live for the build-up, I could hear their cue down the line.

'Let's go live to Carrow Road. Has Delia made you dinner?' Mock laughter.

'Not so far, but we got here early and went up to the Norfolk Broads. It's so dreary, why people go there on a holiday is beyond me.'

My hackles went up and at that moment I finally gained my new identity. I realised I was no longer just a resident of Norfolk. Norwich was my home. Norwich were my team. I wanted to interrupt the broadcast and ask just how living along the M4 corridor was so superior to Nelson's county, but there was no time as our guests had already moved on to stereotypes and further mocking.

'We haven't seen Alan Partridge yet. If things get dull I'm hoping Delia will totter onto the pitch. Let's be 'avin' you.' Neither witty nor original.

Shane Long scored two goals in the last 20 minutes. The commentary went up a gear.

'So long Norwich. We're off home with the three points. Automatic promotion here we come!'

Reading once caused great angst in Norwich by refusing to play at The Nest, perceiving the pitch too dangerous and narrow, although they might have had a point. Their attitude was partly responsible for the hurried construction of Carrow Road. More than seven decades later they were back, causing angst of a different kind.

After the match, the mood was akin to a funeral with home fans and media staring forward with unseeing eyes. I don't remember any booing as the players did their now re-branded lap of appreciation. About a quarter of the home crowd stayed behind, but the away section was full. Blue and white hooped shirts were thrown to supporters who were chanting, 'We are going up.'

I wasn't. I was going to Charlton, hoping for a miracle. On the way home my friend got hit in the face by a Reading fan. Karma ensured they didn't go up and I wasn't really bothered.

The play-off curse has never lifted from the Royals. I don't think any team has a more painful record. The 2017 play-off final defeat to Huddersfield on penalties was surely agony for all those involved but pretty dull for everyone else. And for me, it was confirmation that I'd moved on and moved away because I was really mostly bored by the game.

So, the transfer to yellow and green is complete. And what happens when Norwich City come face to face with my ex these days?

I partied with the Canary Fairy on a pool table at a local pub following the Phil Mulryne one-two with the referee, jumped for joy during the season of late winners as David McNally's quick thinking bypassed the time-wasting visitors, and — best of all — there was the game when my youngest daughter held hands with Iwan Roberts as she walked onto the pitch in a Norwich City kit as mascot for the away side at the Madejski Stadium. She was born and raised a Norwich City fan and I'm confident she'll break the family tradition of switching teams.

So I think I'm just about qualified for naturalised Canary Citizenship. Oh, and I finally met Ken Brown.

'How do we know Jesus wasn't born in Ipswich? Because they couldn't find three wise men or a virgin.'

Ken sounded slightly shocked but laughed — probably out of politeness — at the words he had just read out on live radio. It was a joke from specially made crackers at the Christmas edition of our sports show.

Ill-judged cracker joke apart, he was full of charm, wit, and wisdom, with a plethora of refreshingly non-fence sitting opinion. Our hitchhiker from that holiday 40-plus years ago was quite right: Ken Brown is a really nice bloke, but we already knew that.

Tim MacWilliam, Fellow of the Royal Society for Public Health, runs a company that trains hospitality industry professionals in safety and food hygiene. He is a regular presenter on Future Radio and works with a team providing Norwich City match commentaries for Soccer Sight, a service for the visually impaired.

4

Ken Brown was manager for more matches than anyone in Norwich City history — and his spell in charge followed seven years as assistant manager. Yet, despite serving and surviving for so long in a fiercely competitive industry, he was known for his almost constant smile. It was one of the reasons why he became, and remains, among the club's best-loved figures. Here is his story.

ABSOLUTELY POSITIVE

BY KEN BROWN

My Norwich City Tale started because I more or less had to come and work at the club, or I wouldn't have had a job! I'm glad I did end up at Norwich, though.

When I arrived in November 1973, it was as assistant manager to John Bond and I think people know that we'd been players together at West Ham. I played alongside him in the back four and we got on well — but we weren't best mates or anything as players, just teammates who shared some great moments on the pitch.

It was a decent West Ham side. I got into the team when Malcolm Allison was injured. He had a lot of influence at the club and I was half expecting to be dropped when he got fit, but he said, 'No, don't drop him.' So we ended up playing alongside each other. I was the orthodox centre-back, Malcolm played alongside me, and Bondy was at right-back. Malcolm was the slowest mover you'd ever come across, but he was powerful and strong.

Later on, I played alongside Bobby Moore. I was the centre-back and he was in that role that Malcolm had developed. I can't say that any of us thought from day one that Mooro would go on and captain England and become one of the game's greatest names. He was the most quiet-natured youngster who'd come into the team. He kept himself smart and well turned out, but he just got on with his job. Of course, as he progressed he became a very special defender, but he still always played in that same way — nothing showy or outlandish, just doing his job. He was a great feller to be with and to have a night out with, but as a footballer, everything he did was sort of controlled.

As far as me and Bondy were concerned, we didn't get to know each other really well until we both went to Torquay as players in 1967. We were still training at West Ham but joining up with Torquay for games, and we used to travel to those games together.

John opened a sweet shop in Torquay, and we'd go down there on the Friday so that John could look in at the shop, and we'd play on the Saturday. It was a long old drive — this was in the days before motorways, don't forget. We became good friends (which was just as well considering how long we were in cars together!) and our families all got to know each other from then on. I used to get on really well with John and Jan's children: their daughter Toni and their son Kevin — who went on to play for Norwich, of course. Lovely people.

When John became manager of Bournemouth, in May 1970, he asked me to go there with him as the trainer, which is what teams had in those days. We had a lot of success and got some really good players together — and then took most of them to Norwich when we went there in 1973: players like Ted MacDougall, Phil Boyer, David Jones, Tony Powell, Mel Machin, John Benson. And there was Kevin Reeves, who was an apprentice with us at Bournemouth and then we signed him for Norwich. He went on to earn Norwich their first £1 million fee.

In 2017, when Bournemouth played West Ham in the Premier League, the Bournemouth chairman, Jeff Mostyn, invited me to go along as his guest, which was a nice thing because both those clubs played a big part in my life. In fact, and I have got to be honest, I didn't want to leave Bournemouth when John got the Norwich job. I thought it was lovely down there on the South Coast. I liked everything about it. John said,

'Come to Norwich with me. It's gone well here and we can do it again there.' But I said, 'They might give me the manager's job here at Bournemouth.' But John said, 'You ain't going to get the job.' So I more or less had to go to Norwich because I didn't want to be out of work. But, although I'd been reluctant, my family soon settled in Norfolk and I had a bigger role and the formal title of assistant manager at Norwich.

It wasn't the first time I'd lived in Norfolk though. In the Second World War I'd been evacuated from Dagenham to Burlingham, a village near Acle. We came with another Dagenham family, the Smiths. So the Browns and the Smiths descended on rural Norfolk. The locals probably thought the names were aliases! My dad had to stay put in Dagenham and two of my brothers, Ron and Jack, were in the army. So it was just my mum, me, and my younger brother, Alan, who found ourselves in Norfolk. It was all very different but it was a relief too, because in Dagenham we'd been watching bombs being dropped and had seen aeroplanes shot down.

The chairman at Norwich, when me and Bondy arrived in 1973, was Sir Arthur South, and he idolised John. I don't think that's too strong a word. He thought John was great at his job and great for what he — Sir Arthur — wanted to achieve for the club.

We were following Ron Saunders, who had played a very different type of football to what we wanted. We wanted our team to play as we had at West Ham, and how we'd got the Bournemouth lads playing. People talked about 'the West Ham way', but we thought it was just the way football should be played — with skill and passing, and not kick and chase — and we wanted people to talk about 'the Norwich way'.

When we first started taking training at Norwich, the players couldn't believe that they didn't have to do a great long run. We arrived in the November, so they were all supposed to be fit already, and we wanted to get them working with the ball. But on the very first day they started getting themselves ready for a run, and we said, 'What are you doing?' They said, 'This is what we've got to do.' And we said, 'No you haven't! Get over to the pitch and take as many balls as we've got here.'

Me and John looked at each other and sort of went, 'What's all that about?' They couldn't believe they weren't going running for several miles and we couldn't believe they thought that was what they should be doing in November. It was the opposite of what we wanted.

The training ground was at Trowse, and it needed some work doing on it. One of the first things John said to Sir Arthur was, 'You've got to sort out the training ground.' So he had a new changing pavilion built and spent some money trying to improve the pitches.

But I loved Trowse from the start — because it was such a short distance from my new home and was an easy drive. I lived in Postwick. John lived in Cringleford. It was certainly all a lot more convenient than when we'd both been commuting to Torquay from the London area!

As well as smartening up the training facilities, we wanted a proper youth set-up, which Norwich didn't really have. They only had an A team, who played in the Eastern Counties League against men's sides like Yarmouth and Lowestoft, so we applied to put a team in the South East Counties youth league, which is where all the professional clubs in London had their under-18s. But the London clubs said, 'We can't afford to go to Norwich every other week.' So we said, 'We'll play all our games away from home.' And that was what we did for a few seasons, till they accepted us.

Before John and me came along, Norwich didn't have any real relationship with the schools. They used to send their best players to anywhere except Norwich City. So we appointed a schools liaison officer and I used to go regularly and talk to teachers who were involved with running school teams.

So one way and another we were spending quite a bit of the club's money, but Sir Arthur was as good as gold about that. He could see what we were trying to do and he wanted the same sort of club as we did: a club trying to play good football on the pitch and trying to be as good as we could off it.

We thought, 'You can't just sit back and do nothing. You've got to keep trying to improve everything — the training ground, the scouting, the youth set-up, the players, the way we play. You've got to try and keep trying.'

There were some good people at the club already, though — people like Duncan Forbes and Dave Stringer, who had been at the heart of the defence for Ron Saunders. Duncan could sense danger and deal with it, and that allowed others around him to play. Dave has always been the most genuine bloke you could want to meet, and when I became Norwich manager a few years later, I was very happy to have Dave in charge of the youth team.

But I'm getting ahead of myself. Let me tell you about the period when John was very much the boss and I was his assistant.

We signed some really good players. John used to do all the deals and there was hardly a day when he wasn't trying to sign this player, or asking about that one. He used all his old West Ham connections really well, so that we were able to sign Martin Peters, who'd been a World Cup winner not many years before, and we had John Sissons for a while. We took Colin Suggett from West Brom. We sold Graham Paddon to West Ham but bought him back for less money three years later. We got Jimmy Neighbour from Spurs. And of course we signed nearly everyone who'd been with us at Bournemouth!

Every single one we signed had one thing in common: they could play. They'd all cost millions and millions these days.

John was always wheeling and dealing, always trying to improve the team. He was so intense about everything as well. He would get blooming angry with players if he thought they hadn't tried hard enough during a game. John would set out beforehand what he expected and then if the player let the team down, John would be all, 'I'm fining you!'

My job was to be a foil for all that. So if a player was fined, I would be all smiles and laughing and say, 'That's another few quid you've got to give us.' And the other players would give the one who'd been fined some stick and it would turn into a sort of joke.

I definitely wasn't undermining John in any way, shape or form. He was very, very good at what he did. I always backed him up 100 per cent. But I did see my job as being the one who was less intense — the one the players could talk to, the go-between.

John used to take things personally. If a player had a bad game, John would have a go at the player but would also think it was his fault: perhaps the coaching or the preparation hadn't been right — something like that. He got so upset with himself. I used to watch him, see him take all the troubles and problems home with him and think, 'That ain't right.' There was no point in trying to talk John round, though. He would just go into a blacker mood.

That was just his way, and it did bring the absolute best out of some players. It certainly brought some really great results to Norwich City. But I felt I had to help some of the lads cope with that intensity — without going against John in the slightest — by always having a smile ready. I didn't find that hard because I think I am naturally a positive sort of person.

I did think, 'If I'm ever a manager, I won't be like John is. I'm not going to make myself ill by being that intense.' But I was more than happy being John's assistant, and I was very proud to have been alongside him at Bournemouth and Norwich.

In October 1980, John left to manage Manchester City and decided that he didn't want me to go with him. He took John Benson and John Sainty, but not me and it was hard to take — I can't pretend otherwise. So I had the same worry as I did when he left Bournemouth: that I'd be out of work. But I went to see Sir Arthur and said, 'Can you give me an honest reason why I should not follow John as manager?' And I was delighted when he thought about it and decided I should step up to the top job.

One of the candidates I considered for the role as my assistant was Ronnie Brooks. He worked with the juniors. He loved the club and could sell it to kids and parents as the sort of place they could trust. But I made Mel Machin my assistant because he was like John — somebody who would give the players a boot up the backside. I thought me and Mel could have the same sort of partnership as I'd had with John, and the pair of us would have the same sort of relationship with the players without me having to try to change my character to become more intense.

My wife, Elaine, and I visited Mel and his wife, Jo, in 2017 and she said that Mel had always taken the job home with him. If he had a bad day with the football club, he would have a bad evening at home. And that was like John.

I was never like that. Some people have a trick of telling themselves to turn off their work worries when they get in their car to go home, or when they reach a certain point of the journey. But I never had to do anything like that — and the journey was too short anyway! No, I don't get too upset in the first place.

Elaine says she's only seen me lose my temper twice in the last 18 years. She says it's annoying sometimes that I don't lose my temper — but I say, 'Well let's not argue about that either!'

That's not to say that I didn't hurt when my team lost. Of course I did. But if I thought the lads had given as much as they could, I was able to accept that sometimes you lose football matches. I didn't feel pressure as such. I felt sorry for the players when we lost, and of course, I definitely didn't want to lose either. But I was generally OK. I didn't let any players take the mickey by misbehaving or not doing things properly. I could be strict when it was right to be strict. But I didn't over do it.

So Mel and I worked well together. Mel would put on the training sessions and I would look at individual players while the sessions were taking place. Mel wouldn't always be able to spot what was going on, but I'd spot someone shirking a bit and go up to him and say, 'Listen, everyone else is getting something from this session, so you do it properly too.' Or I would call someone out, saying, 'Hey! You're trying to hide. Get involved. Now!' And, maybe, because I had this reputation for being all smiles, it made everyone take notice if I was giving a player a bollocking.

Some very good players joined the club on my watch. I signed Chris Woods, Mike Phelan, John Deehan, Keith Bertschin, Dave Watson, and Steve Bruce. I signed Martin O'Neill twice! And I signed the bulk of the side who did really great a while after I'd left: the team who finished third in the Premier League and did so well in Europe under Mike Walker. I'm talking about Bryan Gunn, Ian Culverhouse, Mark Bowen, and Ian Crook. Two more of that team who did so well for Mike — Jerry Goss and Ruel Fox — joined the club as kids while I was in charge and had the final say on who we took on. Louie Donowa, Dale Gordon, Peter Mendham, and Robert Rosario were others who graduated from the youth team to the first-team while I was manager.

Bringing kids through was important to me. I made sure that anyone who got all the way through our system got at least one game in the senior team. Even if we didn't think they had a big future in the game, we never cast them aside without giving them one Norwich City game to look back on. I had a wonderful career myself, and I realised how lucky I was, so I understood what a blow it was when a youngster was let go by a club.

Stevie Bruce came from Gillingham and we got him quite cheap because the fee was decided by a tribunal. I went back to Gillingham several months after we'd signed him and their chairman grabbed me by my jacket lapels and accused me of 'stealing' their best player. I said, 'You can have him back then... but it's going to cost you a million!'

Dave Watson was in Liverpool reserves. I got permission to talk to him and he came down from Merseyside with his dad on a coach. I think what clinched the deal was that I said I'd reimburse them for their tickets!

Watson and Bruce were centre-back partners when we won the League Cup — the Milk Cup as it was called then — at Wembley in 1985. So I must have been a fairly decent judge of a player, but I was interested in what sort of person I was signing as well. I was looking for an honest professional. In that Milk Cup team were two more of my signings. They'd been to a few clubs and weren't exactly youngsters, but they were exactly the sort of player and sort of person I wanted for Norwich City: Asa Hartford and Micky Channon.

I used to go in to see the chairman, Sir Arthur, and say, 'I've seen this player I'd like to buy.' Sir Arthur would stick his bottom lip out, look me in the eye and say, 'Can he play?' I used to think to myself, 'If he couldn't I wouldn't be standing here asking you for the money.' But, out loud, I would say, 'I think he'll do well for us, chairman.' And he never once refused me. Never once.

The season when I took over from Bondy, we were relegated. But Sir Arthur didn't blame me and we bounced straight back, winning 13 of our last 17 games. And by the 1984-85 season, Mel and I knew we'd put a decent team together. You can never be sure what is going to happen with injuries and suspensions, bad luck, bad decisions and so on, but we knew we'd got a team who, on their day, would give anyone a game. That was the season when there was a fire in the old main stand, on the Carrow Road side of the ground, and it had to be left empty for the rest of the season.

To be honest, our early performances in the Milk Cup were nothing to write home about. We played lower-division teams and nearly let ourselves down a couple of times. But we made our way to the semi-finals. And we were drawn to play Ipswich.

It was over two legs and we lost 1-0 at Portman Road. The second leg, under the Carrow Road lights on a Wednesday night in March, was one of those very special occasions for Norwich City. There were only three sides of the ground with people in, but those three were packed and I still have supporters come up to me and say that it was their all-time favourite match. In many ways, it was better than the final. There were a few naughty challenges flying about, and there were a couple of occasions when players squared up and it was really, really tense. Channon did some really clever work to set up 'Dixie' Deehan for a shot which deflected off a Town player's knee and then ricocheted into the goal off the post. That was at the River End in the first-half and it brought the tie level on aggregate.

So we were playing towards the Barclay in the second half and attacked and attacked. We kept going forward. We had about five corners and they cleared off their line once, but it got to a couple of minutes before the end of normal time and it was still 1-1 on aggregate. Then Marky Barham put a ball in from the left and it was deflected behind for another corner.

I was shouting to our midfield not to push up too far, because we always sent Watson and Bruce up for corners and so I wanted to make sure we had some midfielders ready to cover if the opposition broke out. I was much more concerned that we were organised properly than thinking, 'This could be it!'

But Barham took a sweet corner and Brucie just timed his run and wasn't picked up. He just ran, ducked down a little bit, and nodded the ball upwards into the roof of their net. He set off on a victory run that he'd probably still be on now if the lads hadn't caught up with him and piled on top of him. Great stuff. A great night.

I'd played at Wembley three times and won three times. I earned my only England cap there in a 2-1 win over Northern Ireland, and I won there twice with West Ham: the 1964 FA Cup final and then, the following year, the European Cup Winners' Cup final. Then I went to the League Cup final with John and Norwich in 1975, when we lost.

To be able to go back, yet again, ten years on, as a manager was a really great thing to happen to me. I knew the people of Norwich and Norfolk would love the occasion, and I felt proud to be a part of giving them that experience again.

In 1975, the team had frozen at Wembley. And I knew they'd done the exact same thing two years earlier when they'd been there with Ron Saunders. So I had to try and make sure that didn't happen to us in 1985. I tried to prepare the lads for the experience. Some wanted me to tell them everything I could. Some didn't want to think too much about it. I treated them as individuals and, with the squad, tried to strike a balance. But on the way to the stadium on the day of the final, I got them all singing. We sang the same song over and over again. 'It's Now Or Never'.

When the 1985 team was brought together by the club 20 years later for a big gala dinner, everybody was staying at Sprowston Manor and got picked up by coach, and as the driver turned the corner just before the ground, everyone burst into song again, 'It's now or never!'

That 1985 final wasn't one of Wembley's finest matches, but we beat Sunderland 1-0 and when the players put the cup in my hands afterwards, I looked around for Sir Arthur and gave it to him. I knew what it meant to him, and that was my thank you to him for giving me the chance to be manager.

The parade around the City with the trophy was a wonderful event as well. And the next game — a Carrow Road victory over Coventry — was a continuation of the celebration really.

But of the 12 remaining games that season, we lost eight and won only two. We were relegated, along with the team we had beaten at Wembley, Sunderland.

And, that summer, there was another big disappointment. As Milk Cup winners, we should have played in Europe — in the UEFA Cup. But a fortnight after our season finished, the final of the European Cup — which is now known as the Champions League — was played at the Heysel Stadium in Brussels, between Liverpool and Juventus. There was crowd trouble and a wall collapsed, killing 39 people, mostly Italians. Liverpool supporters were blamed by UEFA and English fans were banned from all European competitions from the following season — the one in which my Norwich side were due to make their European debut.

I'd gone on holiday by the time Heysel happened and the editor of this book, Mick Dennis, who was working for *The Sun*, rang me the next morning and said his newspaper had been told that the Government were going to stop English teams playing in Europe. So I knew before UEFA made it all official. It was a real disappointment, but it was something I couldn't do anything about at all, and so I just got on with preparing for what turned out to be a successful season.

Before I'd gone on holiday I had called a meeting of all the players and told them they could all leave if they wanted to. I didn't say that as a punishment. I wanted to do what was best for them. After winning the Milk Cup I thought they deserved my thanks, regardless of being relegated. People might think that I was wrong, but I felt that was the right way to treat those players, and I also needed to find out if they had the stomach for a fight in the second tier. So I told them all, 'If you want to leave, I'll put you on the list. You are all good enough to play in the top division, and if any one of you wants to leave, come and see me and I'll see what I can sort out for you.'

Not one of them wanted to go. They still had the passion. But I freshened the squad up a bit, and signed Kevin Drinkell, a striker who'd averaged a goal every three games or so for Grimsby. He was another one I got a bit on the cheap with the help of a tribunal. And we bounced back as champions, with my new striker getting 22 goals to become the division's top scorer and the club's player-of-the-year. From the start of October, when we lost at home to Wimbledon, until March, when we lost at blooming Wimbledon, we didn't lose a single league game in 18 matches. We won 10 on the spin in that run too.

But during the season, while we were winning the second tier, Sir Arthur South was replaced as chairman by Robert Chase and I never had the same relationship with him. Mr Chase wanted to know every little thing I was doing every day. Where was I going? Why are you going there? What are you doing that for? I didn't think he knew much about football and so it got me really fed up that he seemed to be checking up on me all the time. For some unknown reason he didn't like me, and to this day I can't work out why for sure. Perhaps it was because I had got on so well with Sir Arthur.

After winning the Milk Cup, getting relegated, and then bouncing back as champions of the second tier, our first season back in the top division saw us finish fifth — the club's highest ever position at that time. We only lost one of our first 13 games and we had another good run at the turn of the year when we had one defeat in 17. We definitely had much smaller budgets than the teams who finished above us: Everton, Liverpool, Spurs, and Arsenal. Finishing fifth would have taken us into Europe if the ban had not been still in place.

But in the May at the end of that first season back in the top division, Mel left to become Manchester City manager. I couldn't blame him for taking that opportunity and I felt I could build a good relationship with someone else as my assistant. Yet three months into the 1987-88 season, Mr Chase sacked me. It didn't really surprise me. He'd never accepted me as his manager and it seemed to me that he didn't want me anywhere near his club.

I'd ended up being in charge for longer than Bondy. I'd been manager for seven years and, in total, had worked at Carrow Road for 14. I'd been assistant manager and then manager for more than 700 matches. Somebody told me that nobody else has got anywhere near those figures.

I had a break from the game for a while. I went to Shrewsbury and had one game in charge, but didn't want to move my family there and told them I didn't want the job. In the summer of 1988, I took the Plymouth job and was there two years. That was another happy time, and my family and I moved down there.

But after Plymouth, I moved back to the Norwich area. A friend had offered me shares in, and a job at, Lakenham Leisure Centre. My wife, Joan, was very ill by this time, and she passed away back in Norfolk. I've stayed in the area ever since and later married Elaine, who had been a friend to both me and Joan.

When Terry Venables became England manager in 1994, he asked me to work for him for the FA. My job was to go and watch current England players and assess how they were playing for their clubs. I kept my FA position while Glenn Hoddle, Kevin Keegan, and Sven-Göran Eriksson managed the national team, although for them my role was changed so that I was principally running the rule over opposition teams.

For Sven, I went out to Japan for the 2002 World Cup. I flew out on the same plane as the team. During the flight, David Beckham came over with his dad to talk to me and they had a joke about me missing out on signing David. Apparently, when he was 11 and playing for a team from Enfield called Ridgeway Rovers, they trained at Norwich for a few days and played a game against one of our academy sides. This was while I was manager and David's dad said I had watched a bit of the game. So I said to David, 'So you could have signed for a decent club!'

Norwich was a very special part of my career — a learning stage when I moved from being the man who tried to keep players laughing to the man who had to decide whether they were dropped. And of all the places I could have gone, I've chosen Norfolk to live in. After all, I was evacuated here as a kid in the war, and just over 40 years later I was being driven around the city in an open-topped bus carrying the Milk Cup, so I think I've picked the right place.

In 2015 burglars broke in while Elaine and I were abroad and stole my medals: winners medals from the FA Cup and European Cup Winners' Cup that I earned at West Ham, and the 1985 Milk Cup medal I won as Norwich manager. It hurt a hell of a lot. I wanted my grandchildren to have those medals. They can't have meant anything to anyone else. Nobody else could say, 'I won those.' So, yes, it hurt me. But burglars can't steal what I've done in the game or the friendships I made.

I get invited back to my four main former clubs from time to time — West Ham, Bournemouth, Norwich, and Plymouth — and they make me very welcome. I'm still in touch with lots of the chaps who played for me too. Kevin Keelan and Ted MacDougall are both in the States, but always look me up when they're over in this country. I don't seem to have made too many enemies during my career. Before being a footballer, I worked for a couple of years as a wood machinist at a furniture factory.

It meant getting up at six every morning and I chopped the top of my finger off one day, so I didn't think I was cut out to spend my working life trying to make chair legs! I always understood that being a footballer, and then a manager, was a special privilege. So, if anyone wanted to talk to me about it, the very least I could do was to treat them courteously and be as friendly as I could. It's not much to do in return, is it?

And people say, 'You're always smiling, Ken.' Well, I think I've got a lot to smile about.

Since the League Cup had not really taken off when Norwich won it in 1962, it can be argued that the 1985 League Cup success, under **Ken Brown**, was the club's first (and so far only) major trophy. He was Norwich manager for 367 competitive matches, more than anyone else. Second on the list is John Bond, with 340 — and Brown was his assistant for all those.

TRIBUTES TO KEN BROWN

When John Bond died in 2012, mourners at his funeral included some of football's biggest names and much time was spent reminiscing. Elaine Brown, Ken's wife, thought it was sad that it had taken a funeral to get everyone talking about 'Bondy'. So, two years later, as Ken approached his 80th birthday, she contacted folk who she thought might like to contribute some memories of her husband. Here are some of the responses:

Mark Barham (Winger. 213 apps, 25 goals. 1980-87) To my mind Ken was the most successful manager NCFC have ever had — and it was all done with a huge smile. With Mel Machin, he turned this raw lad into an England international. Then, when I had a bad injury, Ken encouraged me all the way during 18 months of rehab. And my recovery culminated in winning the Milk Cup. Thanks, Ken, for all the wonderful memories and becoming a great friend.

Dave Bennett (Winger. 71 apps, 9 goals. 1978-84) He never had to shout and scream to get a point across. A look would come across his face and all the players knew he was disappointed in us. That was enough. I have particularly fantastic memories of the 1981-82 season. We started badly but the turning point was a midweek away game at Charlton. Ken said that the rumour mill was suggesting his and Mel Machin's jobs were on the line. That rallied everyone. We got a draw that night, won the last 13 of the last 17 games, and clinched promotion to the top division.

Keith Bertschin (Striker. 138 NCFC appearances, 38 goals. 1981-84) When I joined Norwich we moved into a rented house. On the day we moved in, Ken was there putting up

curtains and making the place look nice! I thought there and
then, 'I'm going to like this manager.' And I did.

Wayne Biggins (Striker. 97 apps, 21 goals. 1985-88) Every
day was a pleasure but one sticks in the memory: our first game
back in the top flight after winning promotion — Chelsea away.
We came away with a point and you'd think we'd won the World
Cup. After we'd consumed a few crates of Fosters and a bottle
of gin, we dragged Ken to the back of the bus and gave him
the old makeover using Dale Gordon's hair gel. He ended up
looking less immaculate than usual and more like Stan Laurel.

Janet Bond (Widow of John Bond) Browny is just lovely
to be around. When our daughter, Toni, was young, she used
to ask him casually if she could put some make-up on him. He
didn't bat an eyelid as she applied lipstick etc. and then topped
it off with a headscarf. John used to laugh his head off, and had
to admit Ken 'didn't look bad'! I owe Ken a million thank-yous
for everything he did for John and our family. A lovely man and
a great friend.

Steve Bruce (Defender. 180 apps, 21 goals. 1984-87) Ken
gave me my opportunity to play in the top division. It was a
chance others would not have taken — and after I scored an
own goal on my debut against Liverpool, I'm sure he wondered
what he'd done. To this day I try to use some of the managerial
skills I first saw in Ken, especially his man-management.

Mick Channon (Striker. 88 apps, 16 goals. 1982-85) Ken
knew how to get the best out of people and managed to get
a great balance between fun and the football. So many laughs!
I remember that our shooting practice was so wayward in one
session that Ken spent most of the time stopping the traffic

on the road as we tried to get the balls back. At the Christmas party, we gave him a 'lollypop' stick and a white coat.

Ian Crook (Midfield. 418 apps, 24 goals. 1986-97) He always had a smile — except for one time when we'd had a bad result in London and that was the only time we didn't stop for fish and chips and a pint on the way back. As we got off the bus at the Post House hotel to pick up our cars, Ken gave his most angry words: 'Don't ever make me go without my fish and chips again.' Priceless!

Kevin Drinkell (Striker. 121 apps, 50 goals. 1985-88) I have to thank Ken for some of the great times of my life because without his determination I am not sure Norwich would have bothered to sign me. Ken's man-management and sense of team has stuck with me — ever since we first met for talks at a Bernie Inn in Boston, Lincs!

Sir Alex Ferguson (Manchester United manager 1986-2013) I was a great admirer of Ken's because he was always a source of support in my early days of management, plus he is a good man.

Ruel Fox (Winger. 173 apps, 22 goals. 1986-94) I was fortunate to play under some great managers but there's only one who, if I see him or talk about him, I still refer to as 'Gaffer'. That's Ken. He encouraged me to enjoy and express myself without any fear. He was a great father-figure for me, and I shall always be in his debt.

Mel Machin (Midfield or defender. 96 apps, 4 goals. Youth team coach, reserves' coach, first-team coach, assistant manager. 1974-1987). So many happy memories of Ken — like going with him to Gillingham to watch Steve Bruce, who had a poor game. But Ken could see the potential.

Mick McGuire (Midfield. 182 apps, 11 goals. 1975-83) Through astute buying and the ability to turn players from humble beginnings into internationals, John Bond and Ken Brown changed the mind-set at Norwich — from being a club stuck out on a limb to one that became synonymous with competing with the very best. Ken had a way about him that the players respected. Immensely strong-willed, he was never afraid to stand his corner when he felt he was right, but he also had a soft side — and an ability to get the best out of different characters. Above all, he is a thoroughly good person.

Martin O'Neill (Midfield. 66 apps, 12 goals. 1981 and 1982-83) Ken signed me twice for Norwich. They talk these days about man-management. Well, that came naturally to Ken. Yes, he could raise his voice when necessary, but he still delivered his words in a calm, composed fashion. I wish I could have that quality! Ken's belief in me as a player helped bring out of me what I wasn't sure was there.

Terry Venables (England manager 1994-96) Ken and me both lived in Bonham Road, Dagenham, and when Ken was at West Ham, he sometimes took me to watch the games. I remember him and Dick Walker, another great West Ham name, being so smart and always having fun on their faces. It made me want to try to be the same. It was such a privilege for me that I could involve him in Euro 96 as part of my backroom team.

5

Rick Waghorn started reporting
on Norwich City when the most
successful team in the club's history
were embarking on a barnstorming
European 'tour'. But the next season
star players were sold and the club
were relegated. One year after that,
demonstrations outside Carrow Road
were dealt with by mounted police.
Then controversial chairman Robert
Chase quit. Here is the Tale of those
dramatic times, written by someone
with a close-up view.

TOILET SEAT, RINGSIDE SEAT

BY RICK WAGHORN

Bear with me. A little bit by way of context. My first job in journalism was with the mighty, weekly organ that was the *Wiltshire Gazette & Herald*, deep in Rob Newman and Darren Eadie territory with six editions that covered their Devizes and Corsham homes respectively.

I was the Sports Department. The 'highlight' of my sporting year was the Badminton Horse Trials that over the course of those three days of eventing would attract crowds on a par with Silverstone and the British Grand Prix. Cricket-wise, the tiny village of Goatacre took me all the way to Lord's and the 1992 Village Cricket final. Kevin Iles heaved successive, hapless bowlers all over the shop *en route* to a match-winning century. It was an extraordinary knock, like Beefy at his best.

But then these were extraordinary times for Wiltshire's sporting public. And the weekly cub reporter cutting his teeth in their midst. Nowhere more so than at the County Ground, where Swindon Town were busily making all sorts of headlines — for all the right and wrong reasons.

On the field, this was the managerial era of Ossie Ardiles and then Glenn Hoddle; player-wise it was Shearer and White 'up top' with Ross MacLaren pinging 40-yarders this way and that at the base of a midfield diamond, while at the back, Colin Calderwood ran the show.

Off the pitch it was another extraordinary story that would come to dominate my cuttings file when I sought to further my career on a provincial evening newspaper — a story that, looking back 30 years later, proved to be a perfect apprenticeship for what awaited me when I landed that job in Norwich.

The chairman — or rather by then the ex-chairman — was a gentleman called Brian Hillier, a 'colourful' builder. In Lou Macari he found an equally colourful manager, whose joint misadventure I covered in depth in those tumultuous times. To cut a long story short, the pair found themselves on the wrong end of a betting and tax probe; falling foul of both the Football Association and Her Majesty's Revenue and Customs. Both loved a bet — the trouble being they bet on their own side to lose. Which Swindon duly did: 5-0 in an FA Cup tie against Newcastle.

Hillier lost his freedom when, in the summer of 1992, a jury at Winchester Crown Court found him and the club secretary guilty of tax evasion. Macari was found not guilty, although he was banned from football because of that bet.

The verdict was delivered at a lunchtime. On a Thursday. Our print day. 'Hold the front page!' Four editions carried the story and my double-page 'backgrounder'. But the verdict had arrived half an hour after the final deadline of the Swindon evening newspaper. It also arrived two weeks before my interview for a sports job on the *Norwich Evening News*.

I went into bat with a cautionary tale of a builder-turned-chairman sat large on my CV, and was invited to come and join the newspaper who were chronicling another builder-turned-chairman. Robert Chase, though, made Hillier look an amateur when it came to climbing football's greasy pole, to an extent that — decades on — part of you can only admire.

By the time I arrived in Norfolk, in the early autumn of 1992, Chase was in the pomp of his powers. The Canaries had lodged themselves firmly in the top third of the table and would, of course, go on to finish third in that inaugural season of the Premier League and qualify for Europe. Chase had also long since donned his Football Association blazer, and membership of the FA's international committee offered junkets and handshakes a-plenty.

I, meanwhile, had yet to qualify in terms of reporting full-time on the football club; I was your sporting features man — the junior, jack-of-all-trades, filling in for Trevor Burton on the City 'beat' as and when days off or holidays necessitated my being called off the bench. But that all changed the following summer as Neil Custis left his perch at the *Eastern Daily Press* for *The Sun*, Trevor switched to the Norfolk's 'paper of record' and filled Neil's fair-sized shoes, and I became the full-time City writer for the *Evening News* — a post I would hold for the next 13 years.

I can't honestly remember the first time that I received a summons to the chairman's fastness in an unprepossessing corner of the River End Stand. Trevor had the weekly joys of ghosting the chairman's column for the *EDP*; the *Evening News* had the manager's column by way of return — and both of us spent hours waiting for our 'columnists' to be free.

And Chase was 'The Chairman' — or just 'Chairman' to his closest friends.

It is an interesting point. There was a certain aura there that somehow demanded the title, in a way that subsequent chairmen never pulled off. Roger Munby was, for example, always far more a man of the people. He would answer happily to 'Rog'. Alan Bowkett was Bowkett; he never had that much time for the common, Carrow Road herd, but nor did he command such authority as Chase. Everyone referred to Chase, almost without thinking, as The Chairman.

The manager, of course, was Mike Walker, who, for all his other attributes, was a nightmare time-keeping wise. But once he eventually started, it was as hard to get him to stop talking, particularly as relations started to sour in the autumn of 1993.

City were now in Europe and Chase, already walking the corridors of footballing power via the FA, was as happy as a pig in the proverbial as he got to mix with UEFA's grandest at a club level. There was a twinkle in his eye that year, born of a knowledge of just how far his star had risen in football's firmament.

He was a Yarmouth builder — done very, very good. And he matched Walker in terms of sartorial elegance. Trevor returned from one of his continental jaunts for the *EDP* quoting the manager's admiration for the cut of The Chairman's coat. 'Nice piece of cloth that…' was the Walker verdict. And, as far apart as the two got that season, they did share a love of good cloth.

City's UEFA campaign started inauspiciously enough with a first-round draw against Vitesse Arnhem. But the chairman, sorry, The Chairman was intent on thoroughly enjoying this particular ride; his largesse towards family, friends, county councillors, and members of the local press knew few bounds as everyone happily boarded the charter flight to Holland and savoured the prospect of some four-star lodging the night before the day of the game.

Unfortunately, that largesse did not extend to the quality of the return charter flight. The ageing BAC One-Eleven that ferried 57 passengers back the following evening through an intemperate squall had clearly seen better days. The subsequent Air Accident Investigation Bureau report pointed a finger at the first officer rather than the aircraft. Whatever the cause, it over-shot runway 27 at Norwich Airport and ended up stuck fast in the mud, pointing towards Cromer. Given that the passenger list included everyone from the bishop down, the ranks of the great and the good of Norwich would have been severely depleted had the grass run-off not proved quite so soft and accommodating.

Trevor and I became quite used to aerial adventures in The Chairman's company. Our two papers and their respective reporters settled into something of a pre-match routine Europe-wise. Trevor always got the gig to cover the draw in Zurich, while I would do the reconnaissance trip: sussing out the stadium, its surrounds and the preferred hotel for the forthcoming jolly.

This all necessitated flying out of Norwich in a small, twin-engine number with capacity for seven or eight souls. The Chairman would take great delight in moving up front and watching the pilot line up the glide angle lights on his final approach — he was a big kid having the time of his life. And, if truth be known, Trevor and I were having a ball too.

The reconnaissance trip to Munich, however, found all the seats booked as assistant manager John Deehan joined Walker on the trip. So the *Evening News* was relegated to sitting on the toilet for the two-hour flight to deepest Bavaria. Once there, the sleek Mercedes Estate was also precisely one short of the required number of seats. So it was in the luggage area at the back — I don't think Mercedes call it a boot — for yours truly as we headed off in search of the Olympic Stadium and a sumptuous lunch in the landmark Olympic communications tower.

In what would become something of a tradition — well, at least, for the trips to Munich and then Milan — I had been handed an idiot-proof camera by the photography department at the *Evening News*. The brief demanded images as well as words. And so I had to ask The Chairman to pose for a shot of him looking out over an empty Olympic Stadium and again at the San Siro. The beaming smile came naturally; he knew the art of building 'brand' Chase. And as the local press, we played along, little knowing that there was a bubble fit to burst brewing.

Should we have guessed that the Emperor had no clothes? That a club the size of Norwich could ill afford to be housing dozens of guests at the Munich Hilton and again at the Milan Hilton?

I think everyone was just enjoying that ride, and The Chairman was cute in the manner in which everyone became complicit in his spending sprees. I would have been laughed out of the building had I gone to my editor and suggested that we pay our own way and not be so beholden to the football club. Indeed, if memory serves, there was a certain consternation when the football club refused to offer a third freebie to Archant to accommodate a photographer. Given they were already granting two places each to Radio Norfolk, Radio Broadland, BBC *Look East,* and Anglia TV, it wasn't too much of a surprise when they turned that request away. Even The Chairman had his limits.

Besides, there were other guests to be accommodated. County councillors — some of whom might be, coincidentally, on the Safety in Sports Grounds Committee — were seen a-plenty as County Hall emptied for Norwich's European adventures. For the more rural of their number, this was all a great adventure and something of a first — foreign travel! One left his passport on the plane in-bound to Munich. He was last seen face pressed against the terminal glass in anxious consternation as two of Bavaria's finest German Shepherds and their police handlers closed on their quarry.

Victory that night — the first for a British club in the Olympic Stadium —transported all involved to new heights. Jeremy Goss's stunning volley rightly became a moment of Canary legend; Walker's managerial star rose again as Europe proved the perfect playground for the likes of Ian Crook, Ian Culverhouse, Bryan Gunn, and Mark Bowen.

It was a team, individually and collectively, at its peak. With one exception: Chris Sutton. His best years were clearly still to come. But the one-time Hellesdon High School pupil was already beginning to find his feet at the highest level of the game and where, exactly, he would eventually ply his trade would

increasingly come to dominate my conversations with Walker as
we sat in his office ostensibly penning his weekly column.

In the meantime, however, City continued to rub shoulders
with Europe's finest — and not just football's privileged class.
In Milan, on the night before the game, The Chairman's tour
party adjourned from the five-star Milan Hilton for a soiree at
the British Consulate, where sparkling white wine and canapés,
courtesy of Her Majesty's Foreign Office, were a far, far cry from
a mug of builder's tea on a Caister housing development. Robert
Chase had arrived.

But before long Walker wanted to leave. He spied some
greener grass on the blue bank of the Mersey. The dynamic
between manager and chairman had grown increasingly strained
during that European campaign and the scintillating league form
sandwiched in between. Everton away had, ominously it would
turn out, seen Norwich hit top gear with a 5-1 win adorned
by four goals from Efan Ekoku and one by the increasingly
impressive young Mr Sutton. And the $64 million question was
whether Chase would accommodate Walker's growing ambitions.
In particular, with regard to a new, improved contract for Sutton.

In private, as we created his column, Walker would insist he
only wanted to move the goal-posts for Sutton 'that far…'. He
recognised there were limits within which any provincial club and
its board had to work, but he thought there could and should be
a little bit of leeway.

Chase refused to budge no matter how often Walker
insisted that a striker of Sutton's burgeoning talents was all-but
irreplaceable — certainly under the restrictive transfer budget to
which he was expected to work. So Walker walked. And Chase
turned to Walker's number two, Deehan, as a swift and, alas,
pliable replacement. 'Dixie' had many a quality. Second guessing
The Chairman was not one of them.

That summer, Sutton followed Walker out of the door to join another Walker — Jack, the millionaire owner of Blackburn Rovers, for a then record British transfer fee of £5 million. The night before his big-money move North, Chris and friends hit the tiles — right royally. An altercation with a taxi driver duly followed and, in a city the size of a village like Norwich, the 'news' quickly spread, all over the front page of the red-top tabloids.

The Press conference that followed that morning was hilarious. Sutton sat there with the hangover from hell; Deehan wanted to be anywhere else other than watching his salvation as a manager exit stage left, while a perfectly-poised Chairman simply held court with his usual implacable aplomb. 'I think what Chris is trying to say here…' The Chairman intoned, as the local press smirked at Sutton's clear discomfort.

My own relationship with the striker hadn't started well. One of the more challenging tasks required of the football reporter was to guess the weekend's starting line-up. I got ten out of the starting XI right for the opening day defeat by Manchester United that season (my first in the 'hot seat'). But I'd plumped for Ekoku ahead of Sutton — a fact not lost on the Hellesdon High old boy, who refused to come out of the dressing room for an interview after the following 3-2 midweek win over Blackburn Rovers, in which he had, of course, scored two goals. He sent his best pal Ruel Foxy out with a message. 'Chris isn't speaking to you…'.

He would talk when the mood took him, though. The trick was to catch him when the two other 'Bostik Boys'— Fox and Lee Power — weren't about. They tended to stick together, hence the nickname. Prise them apart and each, individually, could prove very good value story-wise. Together, however, they could make things sticky for a journalist trying to do his job.

It was July when Sutton went to Blackburn and the Premier League. It was only three months later that Deehan's increasingly

tortuous managerial reign struck another low: the exit of
Ekoku. The deal was announced to a Press Association reporter
at an England Under-21 game in Eastern Europe where The
Chairman was wearing his FA international committee badge.

Deehan was clearly the last to know as the local reporters
gathered on the steps of Trowse for our usual pre-match
briefing. The blood drained from Dixie's face when Ekoku's
absence was explained; he was en route to Wimbledon for a
£900,000 fee.

Ruel Fox's departure had preceded Sutton and Ekoku. He
had left in the February, just a month after Walker, and provided
one of my reporting highlights. Summoned to The Chairman's
lair with the promise of a good story, I spent two hours sat in
his reception before I was rewarded with a front row seat as the
fax machine whirred into life and details of a £2.25 million sale
to Newcastle rolled out in front of me. The ink on the deal was,
literally, barely dry.

It got better. The Chairman spoke into his telephone.
'Rile…' The Chaiman could never get the name of one of
his star players right. '…I have the gentleman from the press
here. Now, remember what I told you to say, Rile.' I was then
handed the phone to speak to Ruel. So the *Evening News* got an
exclusive, The Chairman got another wodge of cash for the
club, and Foxy got a big-money move with wages to match.
Everyone was happy.

Everybody, that is, bar the supporters and an increasingly
forlorn manager who were seeing their team being dismantled
piece by lucrative piece.

The Chairman did not leave Deehan wholly bereft of
players. The problem was that he did not sign like-for-like
replacements. Sutton, as his striking feats with Alan Shearer at
Ewood proved, was straight out of the very top drawer. Mike
Sheron, signed for £1 million from Manchester City that same
summer, wasn't.

And, for whatever reason, he never settled. Injury and a palpable loss of both form and confidence did for him. Walker's fears were fast being realised. And Deehan was left to carry the can as the Canaries lost their European mojo and, from the dizzy heights of 1992-93, slipped back to 12th in 1993-94 and into the drop zone the season after.

In fairness, Sheron's record subsequently at Stoke stood up to the toughest of scrutiny — 34 goals from 69 league appearances is a fine return. His two from 28 in Canary colours was paltry, and did much to cost both Deehan his job and Norwich their place in the top flight of English football. They were relegated in May 1995, two years after their highest ever finish: third in the Premier League.

Dixie is a decent man and very good company. He simply wasn't cut from the right cloth when it came to dealing with the wiles of The Chairman. Few were, as Martin O'Neill learned later.

Deehan went off-message just once. As relegation loomed ever larger, he gave me a very pointed quote — how he had refused to sell Player X to improve Norwich City's bank balance. That was a front page lead: the manager biting the boardroom hand that fed him. Dixie knew it. And so, having thought again about the implications, he got off the team bus, found me, and pulled the quote. I bore him no ill will. And nor should supporters. The strain of holding the ship together that spring was etched all over his face. He was a good guy trying to do his best for all concerned in the most trying of circumstances.

Chase would test the patience of a saint, let alone a football manager. And yet you will struggle to find one player from that era who has a bad word to say about The Chairman. He looked after them. And the fact that they performed to the level they did, up to and including that glorious European campaign, was proof positive of a happy dressing room, and of a club where the combined chemistry of chairman, manager and players delivered an era never before experienced at Norwich and never likely to be repeated.

Only when the Canaries started to ask a Sheron to be a Sutton, did dressing room belief begin to waiver. As their subsequent coaching careers have proved, the likes of Crook and Bowen, Megson, and Culverhouse knew their football — and knew that once you stopped replacing like-for-like, a club with the provincial resources of a Norwich would slip from their all-time high. Buy enough second tier players and that's where you will end up.

The arrival of Martin O'Neill that summer was designed to reverse the decline. But it's interesting now to speculate why The Chairman invited such a fierce and combative intellect into the Carrow Road fold. Perhaps Chase felt chastened by relegation and needed, therefore, to appease supporter anger with a popular appointment.

O'Neill had, of course, played for the Canaries which always helps; that and winning the odd European Cup with Nottingham Forest. But there must have been a part of The Chairman that knew that the pair would collide.

Martin was, and is, a one-off. He quit his law degree studies at Queen's University, Belfast, for a career as a player, and legend insists that on his days off, he would sit in the public gallery of a crown court listening to proceedings, most notably the trial of the 'Black Panther', Donald Neilson, in 1976. So he knew how to argue his case, and he knew the value of a key phrase or expression. That all meant that The Chairman was replacing someone who was reluctant to rock the boat with someone who, if there was politics to be played, would meet him and match him.

The six tumultuous months when The Chairman and Martin O'Neill were supposed to be both working for the success of Norwich City were a glorious showdown between two, strong-

willed and obdurate men — a bout for which I was granted a
ringside seat.

All these years later, two episodes stand out which measure
the gulf that opened up between manager and chairman,
between Colney and Carrow Road.

The first concerned one of Martin's prime transfer targets:
Dean Windass. The one-time Humberside hod carrier was
proving a right handful at Hull City, grabbing 57 goals from his
176 appearances. More than that, he was clearly a big character:
one who could rise to the occasion just as a Mike Sheron might
shy away from it. And Martin wanted him, badly. 'I want Dean
Windass,' he said at one pre-match press conference. 'And I
want him before the end of the century.'

To a football reporter, that kind of quote is a generous gift.
You can instantly see the headline and you know the impact it
will make — on both a fed-up supporter cheering O'Neill on
and an under-pressure chairman firmly bunkered down in his
corner office at Carrow Road. And Martin knew what he was
doing. He was using Windass as a stick to beat The Chairman
with: trying to force Chase to reveal to everyone what sorts of
fees would be paid for players.

Windass eventually moved to Aberdeen in the December
for a reported £700,000; the likelihood was that £400,000-
£500,000 down would have secured his signature for Norwich,
which was an obvious next step career-wise for the combative
forward. He would have shaken up that dressing room in a
manner that Grant Holt did a generation later.

Chase wouldn't pay that much. But neither would he
be hectored into saying so publicly. He had long mastered
the politician's art of refusing to give precise details of any
situation and of making broad, sweeping generalisations that,
on reflection, meant absolutely nothing.

My other stand-out memory of the Chase—O'Neill
era is of an invite from Martin to join him on a trip down

to London, ostensibly to report on an FA hearing for Robert Fleck. In reality, the purpose of the day was to bear witness to his attempts to button-hole The Chairman about the money, or lack of it, available for players. Martin believed that, in the streets around the FA's Lancaster Gate headquarters, he would be able to corner The Chairman. And he wanted the *Norwich Evening News* to be a witness.

Whether Chase guessed the plan or was simply too shrewd to take a chance of being ambushed, I don't know. But if he took any part in the business at the FA that day, then it was behind closed doors and neither I nor Martin saw him there.

Later, though, The Chairman made a fleeting appearance at a nearby hotel, where the injury-plagued Jamie Shore was signing a new Canary contract. Norwich's 'next Bryan Robson' put pen to paper and then the delighted Chase hurried out of the building, with Martin snapping at his heels, trying — and failing — to engage The Chairman in a meaningful conversation.

That episode summed up the two men. The Chairman simply ducked, dived, bobbed and weaved his way around Martin's lawyer-like determination to get to the truth.

It was a big, big decision on the part of Martin O'Neill to quit Norwich City Football Club in the way that he did. His position was becoming rapidly untenable and, after long thought, he decided his only option was to resign. The Chairman was neither for turning nor revealing. And when it came to winning the signatures of the likes of Dean Windass, The Chairman's edict was, 'It is for the manager to recommend, and for the board to decide.'

And so, for the one and only time in his long and illustrious managerial career, O'Neill walked out on a signed contract. What he went on to achieve at Leicester City is, of course, the stuff of legend. There was nothing to choose between the potential of Norwich and Leicester. The difference was the manager at the helm. And the fact that he was given the licence to manage at Leicester, and the money to match his obvious abilities and ambitions — neither of which were forthcoming at Norwich. Perhaps the money simply wasn't there. But The Chairman never said so.

With Martin gone, Chase handed the managerial reins to Gary Megson for the second time — this time on a full-time basis as opposed to his five-game stand-in routine that followed the exit of a broken John Deehan.

Naturally ambitious, and with a footballing philosophy at odds with playing 'the Norwich way', Gary was always going to have a troubled tenure. He had a senior dressing room to convince to play 'his way' — not easy given the strength of characters involved and the fact that the new 'gaffer' had been one of their teammates until recently.

Gary wanted the ball played long and into the corners, and I have a lasting memory of an exasperated Ian Crook reluctantly smashing the ball down towards the corner flag at the New Den — to where no one was waiting. He looked across to the dugout and shrugged his shoulders like a golfer told to hit a four-iron shot away from the green. He had, 'If that's what you want, there you go…' written across his face.

Crook preferred chipping a more careful ball into the galloping stride of Mark Bowen as the fullback burst into an opposition penalty area. Bowen, too, had a big falling out with new manager. The heroes of Munich and Milan were desperately unhappy as the Chase regime tottered on its final legs.

By that stage, such was the hostility of the supporters and the media — with whom The Chairman became ever more distant and distrustful — that Chase turned to making his own news, with the help of a newly recruited 'media consultant'. Together the two conspired to ensure that their own Radio Canary took to the airwaves on match-day as a rival to BBC

Radio Norfolk. Large speakers were installed in the four corners of the ground to broadcast the authorised gospel loud and clear to anyone that would still listen.

Behind the scenes The Chairman was looking for an exit. That became increasingly clear that summer as various unlikely characters emerged to claim that they were on the brink of a takeover. I was invited to a meeting in the Hotel Nelson with a gentleman who, I discovered, was under investigation by the Serious Fraud Office. And, even in those days before Internet message boards, rumours circulated that could not be substantiated. One meeting was alleged to have been held in the ASDA car park — a long way from the British Consulate in Munich — and there were people claiming to be brokering deals who were probably just seeking to publicise themselves.

There was the infamous day when Carrow Road echoed to the sounds of horses' hooves as a 'Chase Out' demonstration became so heated that a four-strong mounted police detachment was needed to clear the street outside the ground. But who knows what additional pressure The Chairman was under in his office? What we do now know, but didn't for certain then, is that the club's coffers were empty. And so what pressures were being applied by banks and other lenders inside the office in the corner of the River End?

Something had to give. And it did. Geoffrey Watling was wheeled out of retirement to help lubricate a deal as Gordon Bennett and club secretary Andrew Neville worked tirelessly to ease one regime out, and usher the next one in. The nation's favourite cook was eventually invited to dine at the Canary table as Chase exited stage left.

I have a vague memory of one 'snatch' photo of The Chairman leaving his office for the last time in May 1996 — not quite being bundled out of the back door, but near enough. His fall from footballing grace and favour was complete. It was an undignified end to a period that had seen the club storm some of the greatest bastions of European football, playing some of the most compelling football.

As far as I know, there has only been one interview since that hurried exit — with Kevin Piper on Anglia TV in 2010. In it The ex-Chairman said that it was the injury to goalkeeper Bryan Gunn, who broke his ankle in the December, that destabilised the team in the 1994-95 season and so led to relegation — and not the sale of Sutton, Fox, Ekoku, and Mark Robins.

To keep that unique collection of players together might have cost more than Norwich could afford. But did they all have to go in one season? The Chairman believed (or at least hoped against hope) that when he sold players other stars would arrive on the cheap or from the youth team. But some of those he sold were irreplaceable and it would be fascinating to sit down and really talk with Robert Chase now that more years have passed since that one interview.

But although there have been some reported sightings, he mostly keeps his own counsel and stay at his home on Halvergate Marshes. Again, that's a long way from the Munich's British Consulate and top hotels.

Most of the Chase years were good though: good days for players and fans — and for the young sports reporter in their midst. The builder-made-good did make for good copy, even if I had to fly toilet-class to bring home the story.

Rick Waghorn was the Canaries' correspondent for the *Norwich Evening News* for 13 years, and was literally part of the scene at Carrow Road: there was an advertisement on the front of the Barclay Stand with his name on it. After leaving newspapers, he set up the *My Football Writer* website which provides a mix of good writing and fervent debate about Norwich City.

6

As captain, **Duncan Forbes** led
Norwich into the top division for
the very first time and to their first
Wembley final. He was the granite-
tough defender who embodied the no-
nonsense, no-prisoners approach of
manager Ron Saunders. He remained
captain when John Bond took over
as manager and the club won another
promotion and another Wembley
appearance. Now, cruelly, Forbes has
Alzheimer's. But what follows are
his words, recorded in 2008 by Rick
Waghorn for a book that was never
published.

SCARRED BUT NOT SCARED

BY DUNCAN FORBES

Leaving Scotland was a big thing, a difficult decision for me at 20. But I was offered a deal by Colchester and my dad said, 'You may not get another chance to become a professional footballer.'

So I left my job as a wages clerk in a brewery and my dad, my mum, and my sister saw me off from Waverley Station, Edinburgh, one night in September 1961. There weren't tears as such, but they knew what it was all about.

It must have taken 15, 16 hours to get down to Colchester. And one of the lights in the carriage wasn't working, so I'm sitting there in the dark for a long, long time. It was pitch black and when we reached York I thought, 'Have I done the right thing?'

I wasn't the only one who had doubts. There was a chap in the office who used to come and sometimes watch me play. When I'd told him I'd got a chance to play for Colchester he'd said, 'You've got a chance to become a professional footballer? But you're nay good enough…'.

That was what folk were like. And I have to say that Craigmillar, the area of Edinburgh where I'd grown up, was rough. But I was fit and athletic as a boy. When my mother used to send me shopping — we called it being sent 'to get the messages' — I used to hurdle over these big high railings on the way.

We had a football park half a mile from my house and all these lads used to play on a Sunday. They had about 20 on each side. I was only a little lad then, but if someone hadn't turned up they'd say, 'Right, get on then!' and I would play — usually on the wing — and that's where I first started. I guess I must have only been about eight years old or so, and there I was playing against all these men.

I only really started to play proper 11-a-side football through my school and with Craigmillar Boys Club. At the boys' club we used to play table tennis and basketball. And on Saturdays I'd play football for my school in the morning and for the boys' club in the afternoon.

When I was 15, I left school, and that was the year that two brothers — the Alexander brothers — came to my family's house one Friday night, at ten o'clock at night and said, 'Could you play for Craiglea Thistle? Tomorrow? Three o'clock kick-off?'

I can only have played for Craiglea for a couple of weeks when somebody must have seen me play because there was another knock on our door on a Friday night. This chap from Musselburgh Athletic came and said, 'How would you fancy playing for us tomorrow?' I said, 'Well, I actually play for Craiglea Thistle.' But he said, 'Oh, don't worry about that.'

Musselburgh Athletic were what you'd call in England a decent non-League team. In Scotland we call it 'junior football'. It doesn't mean it's for kids. There were some real men that I played against, I can tell you.

By the time I was 20, I had grown and was playing centre-back. We came in after one game and the Musselburgh trainer pointed to a man in the corridor and said to me, 'That chap across there: he's called Benny Fenton.' Benny was the manager of Colchester; he got a lot of his players from Scotland. He'd come up that weekend, seen me play that afternoon, and asked to have a word with me.

So he says, 'How would you like to play for Colchester?' And I remember saying, 'Where is Colchester?'

He told me that they were in the Fourth Division in England. I said that I'd have to speak to my mum and dad. So I went home and I said to them, 'There was the manager of Colchester United at the game today and he's going to come to this house tomorrow morning and see if I want to go and play for Colchester.'

The three of us — my mum, dad, and me — sat up all night thinking and talking. As I say, it was my dad who said I might not get another chance, and so the next morning, the Sunday, when the manager of Colchester arrived at our house to ask me if I wanted to join his club, I said, 'Yeah, all right then.'

The next day I gave a week's notice at my job, and on the Saturday night I made that long train journey from Edinburgh Waverley station.

In Colchester I moved into club digs, a little terraced house at 13 New Town Road, but found being a full-time pro really hard. I would finish late in the afternoon, maybe half past three, and I would go back to my digs, lie on the bed and I would be absolutely knackered. I just couldn't do the training.

The manager brought me in one day and said, 'How are you getting on?' I said: 'I'm finding the training ever, ever so hard.' I thought he would say, 'Oh, it'll gradually be all right.' But he said, 'What you need then is extra training.'

I made my Fourth Division debut for Colchester United at Crewe Alexandra, at Gresty Road. And there was a big centre-forward there, a lad called Frank Lord, who battered me all over the pitch.

I stuck at it and stayed in the team, but Benny Fenton liked to play man-to-man marking and before a game he'd say, 'Follow that centre-forward wherever he goes.' So I used to stand with the centre-forward. He'd go out wide, not do anything, and I'd stand with him — doing as I was told — and they'd go straight through the middle and score a goal.

Somehow we finished runners up and were promoted, and I had seven years at Colchester. I was still quite happy there, and my wedding was in Colchester. I used to go back to Edinburgh in the summer and I met Janette at a dance one night. A couple of weeks later I said to her, 'I've got to go back to Colchester in three or four weeks.'

She made a big old decision to leave Edinburgh and move to Colchester. She had quite a good job, too. She worked as a civil servant. But she went to her mum and dad and said, 'I've met somebody.'

I had to find digs for her in Colchester. We got married three years later, in 1964, and I've always said to her, 'That was a huge decision: to leave Edinburgh.'

I enjoyed playing for Colchester, but naturally when you're in the lower divisions you're always looking up. And to this day, I don't know who recommended me to Norwich City.

Dick Graham was the manager of Colchester by then and he said, 'Norwich City have been on for you. How do you feel about it?' I said, 'Well, the Second Division is a step up.' Lol Morgan was the Norwich manager and he bought me for £10,000. That was in September 1968. But I had to wait nearly a month for my Norwich debut, at home to Crystal Palace, and then I gave away a penalty and we lost 1-0.

Ron Saunders replaced Lol Morgan as manager the following season, 1969-70, and, man alive, was he strong! He'd play in five-a-sides and there was no way you could get that ball off him. He was so strong; he would hold you off. If you started to kick him then he'd give you the old elbows in the ribs. You're marking him and all of a sudden, 'Owww!'

I was still quite quick. So I was able — sometimes — when somebody was looking to play a long ball in to the man I was marking, to get in front of him, take the ball and away I'd go.

But I wouldn't say I was a footballing centre-half. No, I was a bit rough. At the end of the day, each individual player has a job to do, mine was to stop my man from scoring.

At first I was playing alongside Ken Mallender as the two centre-backs and Dave Stringer was right-back. But in the November we went to Millwall, and Dave was switched to centre-back to partner me, and we clicked. Dave always used to mark the small, little chap. I used to get the old, big chap, and I must have broken my nose seven or eight times; I was continually going up to the hospital to get it straightened and fixed.

I used to kid Stringer and say, 'You're not making any challenges for the ball.' But because I would go for the ball, he would read it really well and he'd come round, get the ball, and play it back to the goalkeeper or out to the full-back.

Every team had a big, tough centre-forward. There was Jeff Astle at West Brom, Roger Davis at Derby, John Radford and Ray Kennedy for Arsenal, and at Chelsea you had Peter Osgood up front. He smashed me quite a few times.

Every player you played against then, you had a battle. If they saw you were weak, you'd be finished. So you would, early on, just go through them; let them know you were there. I wouldn't go out to kick a player and get him injured, but I was able to tackle from the back — kind of take the man and the ball at the same time.

I don't think there were too many players who got injured playing against me, but you couldn't have survived if you were a nice centre-half. I played seven years at Colchester and 13 years at Norwich, and I was never sent off though.

The partnership with Dave got better over time. We developed ever such a good understanding. So I'd be marking a man and all of a sudden I'd shout to Dave, 'Here he comes.' and I could just let him go on and Dave would pick him up. And the longer we played together, the more natural it became.

People wanted me to be the captain of the team and I was quite happy to do that job. And I did have quite a good rapport with Saunders. I'm not saying I got close to him, but I could have little chats with him about what we might do in certain situations on the field, and he would give me a little bit of individual attention. He'd tell me he'd seen the opposition play and knew that the man I was marking would do this or that. At that time, Ron Saunders was definitely the right man for the club. You just sensed that. He wasn't a man you could get really close to, but I would always give an honest performance and I think he trusted me to do that.

He rebuilt that team. He bought Graham Paddon from Coventry, Doug Livermore from Liverpool, David Cross from Rochdale, Jimmy Bone from Partick Thistle. And there were some good local lads too — Clive Payne, at fullback, used to work up and down the flank, and Max Briggs used to work so hard on the wing.

Ken Foggo had been there a while when Ron Saunders arrived and had been a fans' favourite on the wing. But he just didn't have the lung capacity to do what Saunders wanted of him. When a move broke down, he'd have to get back quickly, and he found it ever so hard to do that.

If you looked at that team it was a hard team: players who really didn't want to lose. Saunders built that into the team — and he certainly never wanted to lose. And that attitude really showed in the 1971-72 season when there were three clubs — us, Birmingham, and Millwall — chasing two promotion places at the top of the Second Division.

Our last two home games were against Sheffield Wednesday and Swindon. We won them both 1-0 and I scored both the goals. The one against Sheffield Wednesday was at the River End, and the one that beat Swindon was at the Barclay End. I think they had 32,000 in that day. Days like that you never forget.

We had two away games to finish the season, but only needed one win to get promotion. The first one was at Brisbane Road, Leyton Orient, and I often think back to that night. Foggo and Paddon scored, we won 2-1 and I remember coming back on the bus that night and there were all these supporters on the road in their own buses and in cars, and more waiting for us when we got back. All of us players knew then that we were going to be playing in the First Division, the top division, and for me, that was the be-all and end-all.

The following Saturday we drew at 1-1 at Watford — Dave Stringer got our goal — and we had won our division. Millwall missed out, but their manager sent me a congratulations telegram. He was Benny Fenton, the man who had brought me to England.

When you do anything for the first time it is unique — and that is why that team was unique and why Ron Saunders was unique. He took the club to the top division for the first time in their history. I think he knew, looking at the players and the players that he got in, he had a team that could do the job.

That first season in the top division (1972-73) started quite well, and in the November we got a 3-0 League Cup win at Arsenal with a Paddon hat-trick — but I ended up in hospital.

I was waiting with one of their chaps, Peter Storey, for a corner to come over. As the ball came, I jumped and had to 'open' my body to get my header back across the goal-mouth, and he hit me in the chest with his elbow. The rib cracked and it pierced the lung.

It was right on half-time and I knew there was no way I could play on. Arsenal had an X-ray machine on the spot and they could see the cracked rib and the punctured lung. So they got me off to hospital and I stayed in for about a week until the Norwich chairman, Geoffrey Watling, sent one of his big cars up to the hospital in London to take me back to Norfolk. That was really fantastic.

I was out until nearly the end of January, and missed all the Christmas and New Year games. The collapsed lung healed itself. But where they had put the tube in got infected — and, man, that was the worst I have ever felt. The cracked rib took ages, too. Even a year later, if I was doing a really hard workout, I could still feel it.

The manager was keen to get me playing and I had to do this fitness test with David Cross. Saunders said to Crossy, 'I'm going to throw the ball up, you jump up and just maybe hit him with your elbow where the old cracked rib is.'

So he threw the ball up and Crossy elbows me. 'Oowwww! Man alive!'

Saunders said, 'Oh, you're all right, you can play tomorrow!'

I said to Crossy,' I thought you were going to give it a bit easy?'

He said, 'Well, I can't disobey the manager.'

I was fit enough to lead the team out at Wembley though. We beat Chelsea in the semi-final, despite having to play the second leg again after it had been stopped by fog the first time, when we were winning. It was another unique achievement: Norwich City's first Wembley final. But the big day was terrible. We lost 1-0 and I had the best chance to score, but I missed it. It was a header and instead of going for power, I tried to place it and it just went sliding outside the post.

We stayed up, but Geoffrey Watling gave way to Sir Arthur South, and there was no way that Ron Saunders could run the club after that. The two men were just incompatible. Sir Arthur would ring up and say, 'What's the team for tomorrow?' and the manager just didn't want the chairman doing that.

Saunders left in the November and we did think that something special had ended. But in came John Bond and, to be fair, I got on with him quite well. He knew I had been Saunders' man, and he brought in Martin Peters, but didn't make him captain straight away. I wondered if that was because the manager didn't want me going to see him about a move.

He wasn't keen on my tackling though. I'd go through the centre-forward and come away with the ball, and sometimes John Bond would actually say, 'Did you really need to do that to get the ball?'

But to be fair to Bond, he took Norwich up again and kept them there. When people ask me about him, I tell them that keeping us up was a terrific achievement.

He signed some special players: Ted MacDougall, Phil Boyer, and Peters. To buy Martin Peters for £50,000 was the best deal ever for Norwich City Football Club. Individually, I'd have to say he was the best player I have played with.

MacDougall was a lazy so-and-so. 'Charlie' Boyer did all his running for him. But in all the years I've been at Norwich, MacDougall was the best goal-scorer I saw. I remember a game at West Ham in March 1976 when he scored probably the best goal I've ever seen. A diagonal ball came in from the right and MacDougall hit this left-foot volley. Blazed it into the net. Fantastic goal. He was the only one that could score that kind of goal. Only him.

Was my heart more in the Saunders way than the Bond way? Yes, probably. I was probably more happy with Saunders, but Bondy kept me in for a good few games and we did go back to Wembley for another League Cup final in 1975 against Aston Villa.

But that was probably a bigger disappointment than the first time. You had John Bond there, who loved to play the lovely football, and there we were at Wembley. But they get a penalty, Ray Graydon takes it, Kevin Keelan gets a brilliant touch on it, it goes onto the post, comes back out — and we were all standing there like dummies. Dummies! Graydon got to the rebound and scored easily. I've spoken to a lot of people about it when I've gone about Norfolk in the years since and can't explain why we just stood there. We should have been ready. That was terrible.

So we lost both Wembley games 1-0. I'd read things beforehand by people who said that it is the worst place to lose and that is right. You want to get off the field as quickly as possible.

One of the things that you remember about Wembley is coming out of the tunnel and then having to walk to the centre. Then, as captain, you have to meet the guest of honour. And you go along and they greet every player, and you say, 'This is so-and-so…' I found that quite good. And you've got 100,000 people in the stadium watching this.

But then you lose. The biggest disappointment of my whole career was that I could not go up the stairs to collect the trophy and hold the cup to the Norwich City supporters. That's what you'd have loved to do.

But then perhaps winning the Second Division was more important than winning at Wembley. Lifting that trophy on the balcony at City Hall, after we'd got to the top division for the first time ever, was the highlight of my career.

I played a full season for Bondy in 1975-76, but then David Jones arrived from Bournemouth to play in my position, and I made just a dozen League appearances in 1976-77; then three in 1977-78. My last start was in September 1980, in a 1-1 home draw with Wolves. I was six months short of my 40th birthday.

To play at that age was quite good. You're getting the aches and pains, and your back hurts — but I'd looked after myself quite well; if I hadn't have looked after myself there was no way that I could play in the top division as long as I did.

Southport used to be in the Football League and they were trying to see if I would go up there. But I mentioned Southport to my wife but she said, 'Well, you may have to go up there on your own!' I didn't want to do that. I love living in Norfolk. And so does she. We'd have had to uproot everybody; I had my two sons — Scott and Elliot. I made the decision to stay in Norfolk.

Now I think that I've been in Norfolk so long that they probably have adopted me. When I go shopping with my missus in the city everybody is saying, 'You OK, Dunc?' It's good. It's lovely. I have to say, I have been very, very fortunate. I had a long career in football and it's been a lovely life. I've enjoyed every moment of it. It's just a shame that you have to grow old, but that's one of these things.

Duncan Forbes spent 33 years at Norwich City, 13 as a player, seven on the commercial staff and 13 as chief scout. He captained the team at a crucial time in the club's history — when they reached the top division for the very first time, under Ron Saunders, and then when, under John Bond, they set about convincing themselves and others that they belonged there.

7

Di Cunningham is the organiser of Proud Canaries, City's LGBT fans' group, and chair of Pride in Football, the national alliance of similar groups at other clubs. Here she reveals that it took months of listening to vile abuse at Carrow Road, and then inspiration from Justin Fashanu, to make her confront the prejudice shown by some supporters. Ultimately, though, this is a Tale that should make us all proud.

PRIDE AND PREJUDICE

BY DI CUNNINGHAM

L ike Stan Collymore of old, I spend much of my leisure time
    outdoors in the company of strangers: groaning, sighing,
and occasionally — often after a slow build up — screaming
triumphantly.

Of course you know where this is going. This is a chapter
in a collection of accounts of personal ties to Norwich City
Football Club, and obviously these are the confessions of a
football supporter. Nothing dodgy to see here. No frisson
for me at the thought of racy adventures in car parks; I don't
subscribe to 'Never mind the danger' as a philosophy for life.
Frankly that line in football's oldest song doesn't work for me
as a fans' mantra either — it's been taken literally several times,
too often by the defence in recent seasons, I'd suggest.

I love that supporting a football team can transform us
and our neighbouring fans on match days from nodding
acquaintance to intimate companions, sharing the emotional
highs and lows of our team's progress with others. At Wembley
in 2015, many of us experienced the throes of ecstasy together
with around 39,000 others — kissing and hugging Norwich City
fans we'd never met before. It happens home and away. For a
brief moment we gasp or yell together, then shuffle awkwardly
back to our seats, eyes on the pitch again and keeping ourselves
to ourselves once more.

My first Norwich City season ticket was for the seat at the
centre of the front row of the old South Stand — right opposite

the dugout. It was a golden age: a new manager in Mike Walker, stellar performances in the first year of the Premier League, a title fight with Manchester United, and a top three finish that signalled European football. My season ticket for 1993 included entry to UEFA cup games. And yet it wasn't particularly the success of the team that seduced me as a newcomer to Carrow Road.

As a South Londoner, I'd been to the Valley, Selhurst Park, and the Den. When I lived in Cambridge I'd followed the U's at the Abbey Stadium (I confess to stalking Dion Dublin in Sainsbury's once to check what was in his trolley), but I wasn't convinced. Though I enjoyed games, being five feet four I was unable to see much and was alienated not just by the crowd's height, but also by the moaning, cigar smoke and occasional flatulence. So before coming to Norwich I had resisted unilateral fandom.

My pitch side view — wet grass scented — from where I saw Cantona's scything lunge on Goss in close-up and could hear Ruel Fox bark instructions (a bark that did the trick for Sutton and Robins), certainly played a part in my conversion from generic spectator to committed season ticket carrying fan. But the appeal wasn't all about elite, top of the table and European football; in subsequent seasons there was no sense of enduring disappointment or anti-climax. Despite my formative years as a supporter coming in the club's most successful period in the top flight, I didn't feel any entitlement to that elevated position. Once reconciled to relegation to the third tier in 2009, I took a perverse interest in visiting the other St James Park, was delighted to be able to both stand and see at Huish Park, and was charmed by the personalised park and ride arrangements at the Priestfield (less so by the Bescott's lack of under-soil heating).

For me, supporting Norwich City is an adventure. On and off the pitch there's invariably something compelling going on:

the Chase Out campaign, Delia's call to the 12th man, David McNally's resignation on Twitter, Robbie Savage's dive, Goss's volley, Safri's volley, Howson's volley...

And many of those stadium moments I've shared with unknown neighbours. Some names get exchanged (though there's an awkwardness when you've forgotten and can't ask yet again), but there are plenty of fellow supporters who we sit close to for around 50 hours a year of whom we know little other than their preferred team shirt style, scarf design and pie.

Though I treasure my current season ticket spot at the back of the Geoffrey Watling, I never retain it for cup games or friendlies. I take the opportunity to try different stands with a different view. It's not just pitch perspective that changes with seat hopping. Some neighbours talk (or even offer a constant commentary), some don't even make eye contact. There are those who listen to radios or leave early. Some encroach on your seat, some bring a flask, but no drums, no brass, no bell — I wonder if the box office staff warn newbies at Fratton Park, the King Power, Portman Road and the like, about potential tinnitus risk from seats near supporters with instruments. I salute the Barclay End Projekt crew and their aim to engender Bundesliga-style synchronised in-your-face-and-ears displays of fan solidarity, but backing percussion is not to be encouraged.

I moved to Norwich for work, and so was without family or, for a time, friends. But, whether we regularly engaged with each other in a sense that has meaning beyond the bounds of a sports arena or not, very quickly I had a band of yellow and green kinsfolk, and a feeling of belonging that I hadn't felt at clubs elsewhere.

The loyalty and sense of identity was further cemented for me, as a member of Norwich Pride (the organisation celebrating with everyone the City's Lesbian, Gay, Bi and Trans community), when the club honoured the late great Justin Fashanu — scorer of that goal against Liverpool, the first million-pound black footballer, and the only elite footballer to identify as gay — with inauguration to the Hall of Fame on Friday, February 19, 2010. Rightly remembered for his deft soccer skills, Justin is also an iconic symbol of inclusion (and exclusion).

His happiest days certainly as a footballer, perhaps too in general, were those at Norwich City, where he'd grown up, was adored by fans and where, it's been suggested, he was 'out' to some staff and friends. The bubble of success and mutual support didn't travel with him; the homophobic bullying Justin endured from Forest Manager Brian Clough following the record-breaking move to the City Ground is well documented, and soon after the transfer his career was blighted by persistent injury. After a traumatic front-page public 'coming out' about his sexuality in 1990, and then facing legal charges in the USA, Justin took his own life in 1998.

The Justin Fashanu 'what ifs' are irresistible: would he still be alive if he'd remained a Canary, if he hadn't had that knee injury, if he'd had better advice —and of course if football had been ready for a gay top tier player?

It's questionable even now whether the global sport and its spectators are ready. But since that day in 2010 when NCFC honoured, with the highest accolade, one of its most loved players who happened to be gay, the club have been at the vanguard for LGBT inclusion and anti-discrimination work, and if that can be replicated elsewhere then there's no doubt that change will come.

That day not only saw Justin memorialised alongside Ron Ashman, Kevin Keelan, Ian Crook, and all the Hall of Famers, but a public ceremony paying tribute to the player and calling for an end to homophobia in the game was arranged by the club with local MPs, members of Norwich Pride, and Justin's niece, Amal Fashanu invited.

It was a poignant evening with compelling speeches but my overriding memory, which still generates a cold sweat from what might have been, is from the five-a-side game that followed. I was in defence against the team that Amal was playing for. And of course, friendly games are amicable enough, but they should have a competitive edge too. Well that's how I play. So Amal Fashanu, professional model and designer for her own Black Heart fashion house, was gliding down the wing, about to pass to an unmarked goal-hanger. For once I just managed to hold back — and stopped myself launching into a sliding Darel Russell style tackle. I'm not sure Proud Canaries happened in the parallel universe where that clumsy challenge was made on John 'Fash the Bash' Fashanu's daughter.

Proud Canaries hatched on that day. And three years later they fledged when the club couldn't commit to endorsing the campaign, organised by the LGBT campaigning charity Stonewall, to get footballers to wear rainbow-coloured laces to show their support for the idea that 'sport should be everyone's game'. The campaign was backed by Paddy Power, and the Norwich City hierarchy believed the bookmakers' involvement compromised the club's agreements with other sponsors. The board agreed, instead, to officially recognise a supporter group specifically representing the interests of LGBT fans; the first in the country to do so. And even without the club being able to mandate players to wear the laces, seven Norwich City players did opt to put rainbow laces in their boots, the highest number for any league club then or since.

If I'm honest, in retrospect and given that Snodgrass' politically correct multi-coloured boots failed to convert a penalty against Villa that day, which may, in turn, have contributed to relegation from the Premier League, I'd have been happier if he'd worn his usual lace on the left foot.

The question of why a separate fan group is needed for lesbian, gay, bisexual, trans fans and their allies turns up regularly on social media. Often it's a troll asking who isn't interested in an answer. But it's a useful prompt to note not only the progress that's been made in many countries in addressing inequalities and disadvantage for the LGBT community in recent years, but also the areas where discrimination persists. And so long as homophobic language goes unchallenged in stands and terraces, many football spectators will feel unwelcome and even unsafe. There is machinery at club level and higher up the game's administrative structure to address abusive behaviour — signage, stewarding, policing, reporting, punitive or reparative action (although all of that is often poorly used or ignored by clubs and authorities). But perhaps simplicity is the key: visibility can have an immediate and effective impact. There are no 'out' gay players or officials in League Football but in theory there are more than 1,500 people in the Carrow Road stadium on match days who are gay, lesbian or bi. And that's ignoring those fans who have friends and family in the LGBT community. If all of those people could be seen, I'd guess it's unlikely that anyone would use homophobic slurs lightly. So, with the club's help, Proud Canaries try to be visible.

Since the group was launched by the club pitch-side on February 23, 2014, at the game against Spurs, changes in fan behaviour have become apparent — perhaps best evidenced by comparisons of games against Brighton and Hove, a club whose supporters have been subjected to homophobic chants for years. Tweets following the 2017 home fixture versus BHAFC suggested that, in comparison with previous ties, few slurs were directed at the away fans. And those that were audible were challenged or sung over by other home fans.

Another example of changing attitudes is provided by reactions to our pitch-perimeter appearances. Proud Canaries and our banner have generally been well received, perhaps in part because, at the time of writing, our record is appeared five, lost none. And in the 2016-17 season, our march around the pitch came during the sublime 7-1 tonking of Reading. With the majority of fans staying in their seats to enjoy the glorious spring sunshine and contemplate a mid-game score of 6-1, of course we had a rapturous reception!

But back in 2014, a month after we had our pitch-side launch, we had a second outing, as part of the Global Canaries parade at half-time in the March home game against Stoke. And we triggered a reaction that I'm convinced wouldn't be heard these days. Of course we'd expected some antagonism — after all that's why we formed — but perhaps not the degree of violence expressed by one home supporter. 'Don't clap them — shoot the f***ers!''.

The hostile shout was reported on several social media platforms, as well as to the club with details of the guy's seat number. The debate that rolled out online was a revelation: there was little argument, with an overwhelming condemnation of both the comment and homophobia in general. And NCFC management were exemplary in confronting and dealing with the offender.

In the season that we launched there were five reports of homophobic language and all were dealt with by the club with final warnings. Some responded to the national media reports of NCFC's line with disappointment — suggesting that transgressions should be met with immediate bans and 'zero tolerance'. But we all agreed with the club — if this sort of language had gone unchallenged in the past, it was important to give everyone a chance to learn and change.

For me, one of the most heartening signals of the new awareness of Proud Canaries and Norwich City's engagement with the fan group was that in those five instances of unacceptable language other supporters reported them. That took a sense of what is right, courage, and a belief in their club. We know that British reserve makes it hard to challenge, particularly for season ticket holders when it's someone who we've sat nearby or next to for many years, and will almost certainly see again at the next home game.

Much of my conviction as a campaigner for promotion of LGBT inclusion in football came, as with so many evangelists, from past failings. One of the influences in the development of Proud Canaries was my own inadequacy in taking issue with unacceptable language until it became unavoidable at the home fixture against Southampton, on the day following Justin Fashanu's investiture in the Carrow Road Hall of Fame.

The Jarrold Stand season ticket seats my girlfriend and I had chosen were near the back: a bird's eye view, in line with the River End penalty spot. There was a mix of couples, friendship pairings and groups, singletons and families around us, and over the years a few medical emergencies revealed a number of near neighbours to be efficient paramedics, nurses, and medics. The seats behind us were retained by an entrepreneur who offered them to clients. He didn't renew following relegation from the Championship — I guess he thought that third tier football was less likely to impress! He made the right call on the evidence of the first game of the 2009 season; complimentary tickets to a 1-7 loss probably wouldn't have sealed any deals except with customers from Essex. So for the Colchester nadir we had new fellow supporters in the row behind.

Of course memories of that game are tempered now by those of the rest of the season, and we can look back at the game and Theoklitos's abject debut in the English game with wry amusement and satisfaction, knowing that things turned out all right (bloody brilliantly actually) in the end. But at the time I was overwhelmed with despair, embarrassment and sympathy for Gunny — and so I don't remember any interaction with the two men and their young sons who had new season tickets and sat immediately behind us.

But the autumn and winter fixtures found us wincing, exchanging eye rolls, and anticipating with tight shoulders the homophobic slurs that both men used to describe our players, the away team, the officials, the manager, the board... Pretty much everyone it seemed could be deemed a 'faggot' or a 'poof'. Even the pitch was sometimes 'so gay'.

It may not seem a big deal when written down and perhaps it wouldn't be as a one off. But it was relentless, demeaning and disturbing: not just in the disregard for what's ok to say in public, or a lack of awareness that some supporters are gay, but that the language was used by parents in front of their kids.

Neither of us confronted them for months. If it happened now I know I would say something straight away — those men weren't drunk or violent, there were plenty of other good people around and it would have been safe to challenge. The invisible barriers, though, are several. We think, 'People say stuff like that at football.' We tell ourselves, 'I've never heard anyone else object.' We convince ourselves, 'It's not bad enough to report to a steward.' And then there's all the British baggage: don't make a fuss, don't complain, don't embarrass anyone.

'We've been called worse than that,' I've heard a number of times. But that's the point. Terrace taunts are tailored for maximum repugnance, often associating the opposing team and fans with depraved and criminal practices, perhaps drawing on local history or urban myth. Using words describing LGBT people in the same context is pernicious. While young people are at risk of bullying, self harm, or worse as they struggle with their sexuality or gender identity, and where workers feel unable to 'come out' to their colleagues (yes, that includes footballers) there is no place for homophobia or transphobia in football's stockpile of odium.

On the morning after the club's tribute to Justin Fashanu, and before the Southampton game, Norwich Pride had arranged a stall in the Forum inviting memories of Justin.

There was a constant queue of Norfolk people who were determined to share their stories, not just of watching him play football, but about his involvement in the community — as an ambassador for the Attleborough Gateway club, which provides leisure activities for people with learning disabilities — and his patience and generosity: giving autographs, lifts in his sports cars, donations to good causes.

So when the usual tirade of homophobia began at the match that afternoon, Michelle turned round to make it clear that the language was unacceptable. Except that she didn't. She couldn't make anything clear as she had laryngitis and had lost her voice. So what they heard was some heavy breathing followed by what sounded like, 'Beer'.

The men looked back confused and looked at each other. 'What? What's she saying?' She'd been trying to say that we'd spent the last couple of days celebrating Justin Fashanu and now had to listen to their casual homophobia.

I turned. 'Guys, she said — and I'm saying — we don't like hearing your homophobia, please stop.' There were some denials and a 'So what?' but there was no more from them for that game.

The rest of the season, though awkward as occasionally we wondered if they were dribbling spit or worse on our coat backs, was easier. We moved seats for the return to the Championship and were surrounded in the Geoffrey Watling by the best bunch of supporters in the stadium.

I learned of Gay Gooners — an LGBT social group at Arsenal — from friend and fellow fan, Jules, and we resolved to form Proud Canaries as a campaigning force. We knew other LGBT fans who'd heard abusive chanting or comments, and wanted to work with NCFC staff to combat it.

Our plans were fast-tracked by City's reluctance to engage with the Paddy Power-sponsored Rainbow Laces Day. There was a backlash on social media against clubs who hadn't signed up to the campaign. David McNally invited us to meet with him — and the first meeting in September 2013 led to our formal launch the following February.

At Carrow Road, Proud Canaries have been a significant driver for inclusion and anti-discrimination work, as well as an active part of the interactive NCFC supporter network. The group's impact extends well beyond Norwich too, inspiring the growth of similar groups nationally, and has been influential in policy development; as organiser I was invited to the House of Commons to give evidence to the select committee examining homophobia in sport.

The overarching message is that much more needs to be done by the governing bodies, and by the Premier League, Football League and other competitions, to ensure that the good practice seen at some grounds — particularly those which have a visible LGBT fan base — is shared consistently so that we can all expect a systematic response to any abusive behaviour wherever we're supporting our team, and that all fans feel welcome in the country's stadiums.

Our spring trip to the Hawthorns in 2016 signalled a brief respite in the inevitable slide into the Championship as Robbie Brady hauled us out of the drop zone, but my other salient memory from the Baggies game was a protracted discussion with a police officer next to me at the end of our row in the Smethwick End. He was at our end of the metre gap between our fans and the West Brom supporters, and there was a steward similarly placed at the end of the home fans' row.

Once Brady had scored, one Baggies fan stood on his seat, ignored the game, threw the finger at us, and launched into an unyielding chant of 'Faggots'. After a minute or so (my calculation makes that 70 or so F words) I turned to the officer and suggested he do something. He shrugged, did the downwards smile and turned away. So I asked again, and again. Eventually he

said, 'What do you expect me to do?' I read out the name on his
uniform sleeve, addressed him directly and proposed that he ask
the steward next to him to deal with the guy. Of course he did.

When I've told that story since, I've heard a number of
police officers, who do great work to combat hate speech
in football and elsewhere, express disappointment at their
colleague's inaction. My own take is that we should all share
some responsibility. Week in and week out, football supporters
use (or hear and don't challenge) offensive and degrading
language. It's sapping, many of us have become desensitised
— too numbed — to call it out or even recognise that it's not
acceptable. I don't just mean homophobia and transphobia;
you can't travel as an away fan for long without hearing women,
the elderly or people with disabilities dissed, and let's not
pretend that racism is no longer an issue. For some, the football
banter code of conduct is that nothing is sacred, that stadiums
are places where there is no rule that can't be broken. Many
clubs aren't doing enough to improve responses to abusive
supporters, no doubt. But between us as fans, we can do more,
and sometimes that means coming out of our comfort zones.

That shared responsibility governing fan protocol is
exceptional at Norwich City. Maybe it has something to do with
the size of the club, that the board features Ed, the two Michaels,
Delia and Tom, and that Stephen Fry, the most famous gay man
in the world, is a lifelong supporter and ambassador, or that
Norwich as a city has a history of welcoming 'strangers'.

I'm not sure what generated the chemistry, but the interaction
and mutual support of the Yellow Army and its component fan
groups is remarkable. The energy of the Barclay End Projekt in
generating atmosphere and engaging new and younger crowds,
the camaraderie nurtured by the Social Club and their events,
the tireless work of the Canaries Trust, and Forces 2Canaries,
the disabled fan group, Capital Canaries and all the geographic

Global Canaries, together with the many bloggers, vloggers, columnists and pundits shape a collaborative force that is true social capital.

A fellow guest on the day the board honoured Proud Canaries organisers with lunch and seats in the directors' box ahead of the launch of the group in February 2014, was John Hurt. The Norfolk resident and Norwich City fan was a pioneering LGBT ally. As an actor, he disregarded his agent's advice and played the iconic Quentin Crisp — a role and performance that did much for the gay community's visibility in the mid-1970s.

So when the actor's death in Cromer was announced on the eve of the home game against Birmingham in January 2017, Proud Canaries tweeted that we should all mark his passing with a minute's appreciation during the game. The undertaking was shared on social media by the fan family and club alike: Talk Norwich City, Along Come Norwich, Minimalist Footy, My Football Writer, Little Yellow Bird, *Canary Call* and more. At the 77th minute of the game — he died five days after his 77th birthday — the stadium was filled with rapturous, yet dignified applause (from Blues fans too), capped with the chanting of 'There's only one John Hurt' and 'He's one of our own' in the Lower Barclay.

Together we are stronger, and together we can and do make football a more beautiful game. And nowhere is this affinity between fans more evident than at Norwich City, where strangers embrace difference in the name of their club. I may not be an advocate of 'Never mind the danger', but for me there is no question: I'm City till I die!

Di Cunningham is organiser of Norwich City fan group Proud Canaries, chair of Pride in Football and a *Breakfast Show* presenter at Future Radio, where she heads the new-music team. Di freelances as a media trainer, and has worked as a filmmaker, sound technician, writer and Health Service manager.

8

Dion Dublin was a footballing hot
property long before he became a TV
presenter. But at the start of his career
he was released by Norwich City. He
ended his career there too — and the
bit in between was pretty impressive. It
included Manchester United, England
and many years at the top of the game.
So what does he think now about
the club who let him go but then
welcomed him back 18 years later?

SMART SHOES, CLEVER THINKING

BY DION DUBLIN

One of the people I have to thank for my whole career is Dale Gordon. He played a huge part in getting me into professional football at such a young age.

Actually there was someone who tried to get it started even earlier still. When I was a boy growing up in Leicester my dad wrote a letter about me, photo-copied it 92 times, and sent it to every single club in the Football League — this was before the Premier League started. The letter basically said, 'My son is very good. Give him a trial.' We got about ten replies, about five trials, and then about three showed proper interest in me. None of it led to my being taken on anywhere though — and one of the clubs who gave me a trial but didn't take it any further at that stage were Norwich.

But my older brother, Ash, ended up living in Great Yarmouth and I went to live with him. He was a DJ, working in the clubs on and near the sea front. He often lived in flats on the premises and I lived with him. So I stayed above various nightclubs, like the 151 Club and the Brunswick. My brother was the best thing since sliced bread when it came to DJ-ing in the Great Yarmouth area, and it wasn't too bad a life for me as a teenager. I had a good time, don't worry about that! Even to this day I love Yarmouth and go back quite a lot.

Ash was there for 13 years and one of his best pals was Dale Gordon, who had grown up locally and was playing for Norwich by then. Once I started living with Ash, he pestered

Dale every single day, saying, 'Get my brother another trial. Get my brother another trial.' And Dale, being the nice bloke he is, did that. He went out of his way to do that, because he didn't have to. It can be a pain when someone is telling you he knows a kid who is really good. I suppose, though, that Dale knew Ash really believed in me and that neither of us would want to make him look daft.

Dale went out of his way in another sense too — he picked me up every morning from whatever club I was living above that week and took me from Yarmouth to Norwich for training.

I had a month on trial, and did half decent, so they gave me another month and so on, and I ended up having a total of six months on that basis, one after the other — on the huge salary of £80 a week, half of which went to my brother Ash for rent! Dave Stringer was manager, Mike Walker was reserve team manager, and Keith Webb was in charge of the kids' set-up. Webby wouldn't put up with any nonsense, which I appreciated because it helped me understand what it took to be a professional.

I was always a striker as a youngster and scoring goals was my thing. Once I'd got this real chance at Norwich, I wanted to repay Ash and Dale, but I also wanted to make a career in football. I played mainly in the reserves while I was on that long trial. I was there at the same time as John Sheffield, the goalkeeper, who went on to have a long playing career with various clubs. And this was the era when the first-team was legends like Dale Gordon, of course, Robert Rosario, Robert Fleck, Bryan Gunn, Ian Crook, Jeremy Goss, Louie Donowa and so on.

I used to clean Rob Rosario's boots and Bryan Gunn's boots, and they were both good to me. Flecky was another who was top class. Gossy and Chippy Crook were superb. Dale was a bit of a tight-arse, but he couldn't help it!

There were some seriously good players and there was plenty of stick flying about, but that just made you stronger, and I loved it. It made me want to be in the first-team dressing room as a player, and not as a youngster collecting the boots to clean. When, later in my career, I was in first-team dressing rooms by right, all the rituals that I had been through — cleaning boots, mopping floors, cleaning toilets and showers — made me appreciate it all the more. It wasn't a punishment. It was to make you realise you couldn't walk into the first-team room without earning the right. It would be impossible to reinstate that sort of thing now, but I don't think you will find one player from my generation or older who will say anything other than it was a good thing, a good process, a good lesson. And, silly or not, to this day I never wear dirty footwear: shoes or trainers. I gained, and still have, a pride in making my footwear as clean and polished as possible.

It was a good era for Norwich, when you look back. Dave Stringer was a very straight sort of bloke and a successful manager, but one day he said to me, 'Well done, but you are not quite good enough yet to get into my first-team squad and so I am going to let you go. But I do know that Cambridge United want you.' It was the end of the 1987-88 season. I was just 19 and it was a disappointment.

When we see each other now, Dave says, 'I know, I know, I should have kept you!' Every single time I bump into him he says, 'I hold my hands up. I got it wrong.' But when he did let me go, he had already sorted something out for me by talking to Cambridge and I went there. Cambridge were interested because fortunately they'd had a scout watching at one of my better games — when I had scored two goals for Norwich reserves against Crystal Palace reserves. The significance of that was that in goal for Palace was the legend Les Sealey, which made my goals very special indeed.

I was gutted when I had to leave Norwich, but the manager had to make a call about my future, and he made it and stood by it. So I went to Cambridge and had to have a think about myself. 'Why did Norwich think I wasn't going to make it? Was that a blip? But, OK, Cambridge do think I can do it, so thank you very much for the opportunity. I shall show you how good I am.'

I got a month's contract at Cambridge, on £80 a week again, out of which I still had to pay for digs and all my other living expenses. And unfortunately Dale wasn't there to drive me to and from training! So I had to learn to manage my own finances.

It was the 1988-89 season. At the end of the first month I got another month, and so on, just like it had been at Norwich. I had a very short spell on loan at Barnet but when I returned to Cambridge I got my first start in the local derby at Peterborough — and scored a hat-trick. I can't really remember any of my goals that day. They were probably all 40-yarders! But I certainly know that it was the following day that the manager, Chris Turner — God rest his soul — gave me an 18-month contract.

The following season John Beck took over as manager in the January and we reached the quarter-finals of the FA Cup, which was a massive thing for a Fourth Division club. And then we got into the promotion play-offs. I scored in the semi-final second leg at Maidstone and made a little bit of history in the final against Chesterfield. It was the first year the play-off finals were at Wembley, the Fourth Division final was the first one, and I got the only goal about 15 minutes before the end; so I was the first scorer in a play-off final at Wembley.

I was Cambridge's joint top-scorer with 21 goals that season, and that goal at Wembley was definitely one of my career highlights. It was about our 58th game of the season and we had all worked hard on and off the pitch all season. I have a saying: 'It is the things that people don't see that get rewarded.'

I went into the gym when people weren't aware of it, stayed on the pitch doing extras — doing the things people don't see, which we all did. And when we won that final at Wembley I felt it was our reward.

The season after that (1990-91) I got 21 goals again and was the club's top scorer out on my own. We repeated the feat of reaching the last eight of the FA Cup and had a brilliant end to the season as we went from tenth place to top and stayed there to win the title and a second successive promotion.

It was a fantastic time to be at Cambridge and the next season we went really, really close to a third promotion but we lost heavily to Leicester in the play-off semi-finals — and that summer Cambridge accepted a £1 million bid for me from Manchester United.

So I have a lot of people to thank: Chris Turner, John Beck, and also Gary Johnson, who was reserve team manager when I arrived at Cambridge and then stepped up to assistant manager when John Beck became the gaffer — plus Graham Scarff, who looked after the kids. Those guys helped me go from being a player released by Norwich to become a seven-figure signing for Sir Alex Ferguson at Old Trafford. So it wasn't just me. It was down to my coaches and their belief in me.

It was at Cambridge, under the guidance of Messrs Turner, Beck, Johnson, and Scarff, that I started to get a feel for what was needed to be a proper pro. I got into the routine and understood what I should eat and drink, and how I should train. I became a man very quickly and learned what I needed to do to get the best out of myself. And I learned what not to do. I became smart, like my shoes. I learned not to take the mickey out of the opportunity or my job. They had taken a gamble on me at Cambridge and I wanted to repay them by scoring goals.

So I found myself at Manchester United as the Premier League began. I made my debut in the fourth game of the season — at Southampton, in Sky's first *Monday Night Football* match — and scored the only goal, a couple of minutes from the end.

It had been quite a journey, as they say on *X Factor* — from being released by Norwich, via monthly contracts at Fourth Division Cambridge, to scoring on my Manchester United debut. But it actually involved messing up another journey: United flew to Southampton on the Sunday but I missed the flight. When I spoke to Sir Alex he told me to fly down on the Monday and I got dogs' abuse from the other players — which was expected — when I eventually arrived at the hotel in the afternoon only a few hours before the game. But when it came to the match, they were all really supportive beforehand, saying things like, 'You'll be fine, big man. You'll score tonight.' So when I did score, it was pretty special. It was a tap-in from three-yards — I was deadly from that distance! — and that memory will never leave me.

Then, the very next week, I started the Old Trafford game against Crystal Palace and a minute before half-time I broke my leg. It was a tackle from behind, and the impact dislocated my ankle and broke my fibula.

If ever you hurt someone on a football field by mistake, you always apologise. Or you get a message to the other person and say, 'I hope you get fit soon.' But the person who did that to me never ever said a word to me. Lots of the other Palace lads, including Ian Wright, Mark Bright, John Salako, and the now England manager Gareth Southgate, all came over and some of them came to the hospital to see me. So I won't even name-check the person who did it to me.

It was while I was out of action with the broken leg that I started playing the saxophone. My dad was an accomplished bass guitarist, and my three brothers all play instruments, but I hadn't ever had enough time to learn anything — until I was forced to spend time sitting about because of the broken leg. I really grew to love the sax.

There was never any doubt in my mind that I would come back from the injury. But it was incredibly painful. And from start to finish I was out for about eight months. I was in a cast for six months. While I was out of the side, United bought Eric Cantona — you had big boots to fill, Eric!

So, by the way, I consider myself the catalyst for Manchester United's success. If I hadn't broken my leg, they wouldn't have signed King Eric. But they did, and went on to win the League. It was their first title for 26 years and the start of the period when they dominated the Premier League. The Premier League did give me a winners' medal, although I did not play again that season after my injury. The following season, I made a handful of appearances and got a couple of goals, but just after the start of the season after that, I was sold to Coventry.

At Coventry I got back to playing regularly — alongside some ludicrously talented players, plus Darren Huckerby! — and I started scoring regularly again. My partnership up front with Hucks worked really well and we had some other great, attack-minded players. And in midfield we had Gary McAllister. I don't think I ever saw him misplace a pass. But we shipped a lot of goals too, and in the 1996-97 season we found ourselves in a real relegation scrap. I scored a last minute winner at Anfield, then got another goal as we beat Chelsea at our place in the next match, but we were still in the bottom two on the last day of the season and needed to win at Spurs — and hope against hope that other results went our way as well. I scored in the first half but somebody called Paul McVeigh equalised and it looked like we were doomed. But then Paul Williams grabbed us a second goal, and right at the death big Steve Ogrizovic pulled off a magical stop and we had saved our Premier League lives.

I learned a lot from the coaching of Gordon Strachan and it was at Coventry that I got into the England team. I won four caps, but there was a little bit of competition from a few other half-decent strikers: Alan Shearer, Michael Owen, Robbie

Fowler, Teddy Sheringham, Les Ferdinand, Ian Wright… Paul Scholes was playing as a striker then. I don't think England have had as many strikers to choose from since that period. There was a ridiculous amount.

Glenn Hoddle was the manager and he said, 'If you were a centre-half, Dion, you'd have played 50 times for your country.' But I'm not bitter or anything. I just missed out on going to the 1998 World Cup in France, but I can say I walked out at Wembley with the number nine on my back, and that is another indelible, precious memory.

My next club was Aston Villa, where I spent six years. I started my Villa career with seven goals in three games, and had some good times with them. In 2000 I scored in a penalty shoot-out in an FA Cup semi-final to take the team to Wembley and I played in the final against Chelsea. I would say I was very fortunate at Villa.

There was the occasion I broke my neck though. That was in a game against Sheffield Wednesday in December 1999, and I have been told that I could have died, or have been left in a wheelchair. I had a titanium rod put in my neck to hold three vertebrae together and was out for three months — but when I came back I helped Villa reach that FA Cup Final. So, really, I'd have to say I was definitely fortunate at Villa because I'm still here to talk about it, and still able to walk about in houses on TV.

And, to be serious for a moment, just how lucky I have been was brought home to me by the death of my very good friend, Ugo Ehiogu, while I was putting this Tale together. We were teammates at Villa and played together in the FA Cup Final. He was a warrior of a centre-back, but an absolute gent off the pitch. It was shocking when he died in April 2017 after a cardiac arrest. He was only 44, and died the day before my 48th birthday.

After my Villa days came a spell at Leicester, and that was where I felt the most pressure, I would say. It was my home-town club and I knew that if there was a crowd of 25,000 I would have seen about 20,000 of them out and about in my lifetime and probably knew several thousand. And there was the added pressure that all my family were at games. I did not want them to hear fans getting on my back if things weren't going well, so I felt a need not to put my relatives in a difficult position. But I thrive on pressure and actually like playing in that situation.

In January 2006 I had the opportunity to link up with Gordon Strachan again, this time at Celtic. It was an absolute pleasure to do so. He was completely straight with me. He said, 'I want you to sit on the bench and come on and play up front or in defence when I need you. And the reason I want you here to do that is that I need someone on the bench that I can trust.' As soon as he said that word 'trust', I knew I had to go to Glasgow.

In my entire career at professional clubs, I must have made getting on for 700 appearances in all competitions. And I would guess that maybe 150 of those were at centre-back as opposed to centre-forward. I was always primarily a striker, but I went into defence if that was where I was needed. And when I played at centre-back I used to think as a centre-forward. By that I mean that if I was marking someone I would think, 'If I was attacking, where would I make my run to get a scoring opportunity now?' Or I would think, 'As a striker, where would I want the next centre to go?' Then I would switch my brain back into defensive mode and get myself in a position to deal with the run or the cross. And with that anticipation, I could normally get there first. I was playing in defence but using the thought process of an attacking player.

It was Nigel Worthington who signed me for Norwich after five months in Scotland. It was September 2006, and I was 37. Norwich were starting their second season in the Championship after relegation from the Premier League. He said, 'I want you to spend a couple of years with me, and bring your experience to our dressing room.' I know there were supporters, and perhaps some people at the club in Norwich, who asked, 'What are we signing him for? He's had his time.' I don't mean they thought I was useless, or that they questioned my motives for joining Norwich. Nobody associated with the club disrespected me at all, but I am sure there were questions about the wisdom of signing a 37-year-old.

I would like to believe, though, that I showed by my attitude in every single game that I hadn't gone there just to top up my pension. And, if I did persuade the fans that I was there to do my absolute best for Norwich City, then that is because of the work ethic I learned all those years earlier as a youngster at the club. I had been shown that you have to earn the right to be a professional footballer, and I never ever played the game in any different way to that. I never took my profession for granted or disrespected it.

I suppose it's a bit like my shiny shoes: it's about professional pride and not having a lazy approach. So, when I crossed that white line and went onto a pitch, I was going to work. If that meant you and I were going to kick each other all day, I'd get on with doing it. I would do my job. If I had to go through someone to get a goal, I would do it. If I had to put my head in to stop someone scoring, well, that's my job and I'd do it. I'll take a broken nose if I have to take it to score. Totally committed.

That's how I always was, and it started at Norwich, so I was so happy to get the incredible opportunity to go back there after all that had happened to me — to finish the circle. It felt like the perfect last chapter. It felt complete.

It was great to play with Mr Huckerby again and to join a group of players who accepted me and looked after me. I don't think the fans saw how the players were more than prepared to do my running if they could see I was knackered, and let me concentrate on doing what I could still do. And if things weren't going well for me, they would help me out. There was never any suggestion of leaving me exposed. I think they could see my professional attitude and determination and they were ready to match it, and that was a wonderful thing to share at that stage of my career. They knew that if the gloves had to come off I would be there for them, and so they always had my back covered — always.

I was captain a lot of the time, and loved that. And the other senior players, guys like Hucks, totally accepted that, which was lovely. I think that in nearly all the photographs of me playing in that second spell at Norwich there is a smile on my face. It was genuinely a fabulous time for me.

Except the results. They weren't good enough. And the man who signed me, Nigel, was sacked very soon afterwards! Peter Grant had a year in charge and then we had a great escape from the threat of relegation under Glenn Roeder. When he had taken over from Peter, Norwich had looked very likely to go down, but we rallied under Glenn, and by the time the last game of the season arrived, at Sheffield Wednesday, we were safe.

By then, I had announced that I would not be seeking to stay at Norwich or to play anywhere else. It was time to stop. My body had told me, and I had then told everyone else.

It was a tough decision to make because the club offered me another year. Players like Darel Russell and Dickson Etuhu made a point of saying they hoped I would stay. But I knew they weren't feeling all the creaks and aches that I was feeling. I was 39 and had to get into training a lot earlier than guys like those two did, just so that my old bones would function.

I used to get in an hour and a half before training started. I had to stand in a hot bath for 45 minutes. Jo Saunders was the masseuse and she'd run the bath and I'd keep my knees and Achilles tendons submerged before she could give me a massage. Then Neal Reynolds, the physio, would put strapping on me, and then I would go out and do my own warm-up for half an hour. Then I would get one of the kids to ping a ball about with me, so when the other lads came out to warm up, I was already sweating and mobile enough to join in with them.

I'd had the broken leg, broken neck, a double hernia, and had broken my nose three times. I think my body was entitled to say, 'That's enough, Dion.'

The actual finish, at Hillsborough in that last game of the 2007-08 season, was definitely the finest finale I could possibly have had. As players, we all knew it was Darren Huckerby's last game for Norwich too, but nothing had been announced and so there was no big send-off for him. That was bizarre because in any list of great Norwich City players, covering the whole time that the club has existed, Darren Huckerby would have to be in it.

But my final moments could not have been better staged. There was a full house at what is one of the game's great old clubs, Norwich fans were filling one end, as they always did, and the manager was good enough to take me off before the end to give me my big finish. I got a standing ovation from both sets of fans, which was extraordinary. There were tears, but I held them back and tried to take it all in. Mark Clattenburg was the ref. Rather than hurry me off to allow the substitution, he joined in the applause. I clapped all four sides of the ground, and I saw that the directors' box had stood up and so had the away dugout. And the Norwich fans were roaring, 'Di-on! Di-on! Di-on!' Wow. I was blown away and I am not at all embarrassed to say that I have kept it on video.

I nearly returned to Norwich as part of the management team when Bryan Gunn took over. He'd become caretaker manager when Glenn Roeder was dismissed and then applied for the job full-time. Paul Ince applied for the job too, and although I was under contract with Sky TV as a pundit, I went with Paul to London and met Norwich people with a view to Paul being manager and me being his assistant. But the Norwich board decided to give Gunny the job and wanted me to work with him. I told Paul, and he said I should go for it. So Gunny and me met Delia and all the hierarchy, and it was all done and dusted — I was Gunny's assistant. But then Sky said, 'No chance. You're under contract to us.' So that was the end of my managerial stint.

I think I could have had some sort of career on the coaching side of football, or stayed in the game in some capacity, because I played in all four divisions. I'd done it all. But my life went in another direction — first with talking about football on radio and television, and then into other areas of television. It's hectic but fun, and I don't spend my time thinking about what might have been. I believe that, in my life, I got the very best out of the cards I was dealt.

I played for eight clubs and scored on my debut for five of them: Cambridge, Manchester United, Coventry, Aston Villa, and Millwall (where I went on loan for a spell while I was on Villa's books). I wasn't always an angel — as Robbie Savage will tell you. I was sent off for head-butting him when I was at Villa and he was at our local rivals, Birmingham. I couldn't moan about being dealt that card: a red one.

There's one thing I'd like to know though. If the cards had fallen a little differently, what would have happened? What would have happened if I hadn't broken my leg when I did at Manchester United? I went on to be a golden boot winner in the Premier League and score quite a few goals for other clubs. So, if I hadn't been injured when I was, would I have scored a few for United? Might I have been there for ten years, or two? I do wonder, 'Could I have been a United legend?'

But that's not a regret, it's just something I wonder. I broke my leg and things went on to happen in the way they did, and

I know I have been very, very fortunate. At the very beginning, perhaps, as they say in the property business, I was a fixer-upper that needed a bit of work. But I did that work myself, with the help of people I have mentioned. And despite quite a lot of damage, I am pleased to report that the structure is still sound.

It began at Norwich, and although they let me go, I learned lessons there that stayed with me. It ended at Norwich too, which was remarkable and fabulous. And so, I am indebted to Norwich City an enormous amount.

After being released by Norwich as a teenager, **Dion Dublin** played for Cambridge, Manchester United, Coventry, Aston Villa, Leicester, Celtic, and England, before re-joining the Canaries and scoring 12 goals in 70 appearances. His many current interests include working as a presenter on TV's *Homes Under The Hammer*.

9

Dale Gordon is one of our own. He
first trained with the club at eight,
made his debut at 17, and was in City
teams who finished fifth and fourth in
the top division. But what about his
nickname? And why was he banned by
England? It's all in his Tale: the story
of the kid from Caister who became a
Norwich Hall of Famer.

I SHOULD HAVE HAD A KEBAB

BY DALE GORDON

Where should I start? I know some Norwich fans still use my nickname, 'Disco', if they mention me. And I know there's the story about when my Norwich teammate Robert Rosario and I got into trouble for breaking a curfew while we were away with England under-21s. To be honest, that night was like a scene from the film *Mike Bassett England Manager*, and I will tell you about it. But I did play a bit of football too! So can I start there?

Growing up in Caister, I used to drive my mum and dad mad because they had to seed the back garden two or three times a year. From age six I used to wear the grass away by playing with a football. I was out in the back garden with a ball all the time — when I wasn't using the playing field in the middle of Caister.

The playing field is still there to this day. A group of my mates would turn up and it was literally 'jumpers for goalposts' until it got dark. Caister F.C. used to play there on a proper pitch. And at half-time in their games me and my mates would be on the pitch smashing balls into the back of their net.

In all the kick-about games I played with guys who were a couple of years older than me, and when I started playing for my school, I always played in an age-group one or two years older than I actually was. At Caister Middle School, the PE teacher was Cameron Newark — a big Norwich City fan — and he was a big influence on my career.

My dad was so passionate about my career too. People said he was too pushy with me, but it worked both ways because I wanted always to impress him with my football.

At my middle school I was in a team who didn't lose a game for two years. We got to a cup final, against Peterhouse School from Great Yarmouth. Ken Brown, who was assistant manager at Norwich City, came to watch the final and I scored a hat-trick, including one straight from a corner. When Ken did the presentations, he invited our whole team for trials at the old training ground at Trowse — so my first Norwich trial was when I was eight. I turned up in an Ipswich Town kit. Yeah, I know. But they were my team then.

There used to be benches against the wall, either side of the door to the changing rooms. I sat there in my Ipswich kit and John Bond, the manager, drove more or less right up to the door and he saw me sitting there in the classic Ipswich Adidas kit.

My dad's family lived in Suffolk, my dad used to take me to watch Ipswich. We'd get a coach from Lowestoft. This was the era of Paul Cooper, George Burley, John Wark, Paul Mariner and so on. I remember sitting at home watching the 1978 Cup Final, Ipswich against Arsenal, and crying with joy when Ipswich won.

But it was Norwich who gave me that trial and they asked me to go to Trowse once a week. Ronnie Brooks was the chief scout, and he used to pick me up and take me home because my dad didn't drive.

I played for England schoolboys, and again was from a younger age-group than most of the boys in the team. I got sort of growing pains in my knee though, when I was 13, and missed a year in the England team. But a lot of clubs wanted to sign me.

It was when I was 13, in 1980, that John Bond went from Norwich to Manchester City, and took youth team coach John Sainty with him. They tried to sign me to take me to Maine

Road. Chelsea and West Ham wanted me too. So did QPR, who were a good side in those days.

Manchester City offered my parents £35,000 and a house to re-locate to Manchester. But Norwich had a good youth system and a reputation for giving youngsters a chance. They'd had Justin Fashanu and his brother, John, come through the ranks. And they pulled out all the stops to keep me.

For me, it wasn't about money. It was about my dad's job, and about my brothers and sisters. My family was settled and I was happy, so I stayed. Ken Brown, who had seen me in that schools cup final, took over from Bond as manager, and Dave Stringer became youth team coach. I signed schoolboy forms at 14, and then at 16 signed apprentice forms. I had to clean Martin O'Neill's boots. I remember they were the Pony brand.

At 16 I was playing for England under-18s. We played Wales at Doncaster, and I wore Martin O'Neill's boots. Don't ask too many questions! He wasn't best pleased because he had no boots to wear in training.

By 1984, when I turned 17, I didn't spend a lot of time with the youth team. I was around the first-team all the time. Being an apprentice meant I still had to do chores, like sweeping the stands at Carrow Road after matches. But in the summer that year, the first-team went on tour to Sweden, and I went along as the kit skip boy. I trained with the first-team on that tour. This was the time when they had Steve Bruce, Dave Watson, Chris Woods, Peter Mendham, John Deehan and the like. And I actually played in a first-team match in Sweden.

I also picked up my nickname on that tour. After every game, the team we played put on a little celebration. There would be a nice buffet and the likes of myself and Louie Donowa would do a little bit of dancing. Louie fancied himself as a bit of a DJ and would do hip-hop dancing and the lads would say, 'Come on Dale, show us what moves you have got.' So I would be leaping about like an idiot and it was Tim Sheppard, the physio, who Christened me 'Disco'.

Back home in Caister I was good friends with Ashley Dublin — Dion's big brother — who was DJ-ing in Great Yarmouth clubs. Us two, and a black guy called Winston, were known as the Three Degrees, inevitably I suppose because there weren't too many other black faces around. Actually my dad is South American and my mum is from East Dereham.

When we got back off the Sweden tour, the first-team had a few injuries and I played in pre-season games at Cambridge and Peterborough. And when the 1984-85 season started, Ken Brown gave me the nod to play in the very first game, at home to Liverpool. A few slightly older players made debuts that day too: Jan Molby and Paul Walsh for Liverpool, and Steve Bruce for us. Steve headed an own goal and Kenny Dalglish put Liverpool 2-0 up, but I put over a cross from the right that led to Peter Mendham scoring. John Deehan had a penalty saved but Keith Bertschin made it 2-2 early in the second half. Phil Neal's penalty gave them the lead again, but we got a penalty in the very last minute, and Mick Channon made it 3-3. I was 17 and seven months; it was quite a start.

My second game for the first-team was at Highfield Road against Coventry and the man marking me was Stuart Pearce, who wasn't nicknamed Psycho because he liked Hitchcock films. That experience left its mark on me. So did he.

But it didn't faze me, playing in the top division as little more than a kid. I was completely used to playing with and against people who were older than me, so I didn't really think about that element.

I played 27 games that season. Physically I was strong enough and I was quick. But mentally, it took its toll. It was very demanding. I signed my first pro contract and was taken off apprentice duties, and grew up really quickly.

I wasn't in the side when they won the Milk Cup. But I was on the bench in my grey Pierre Cardin suit, with flared trousers that were about six inches too short.

Ken was a good manager. He was the calm one, and his assistant, Mel Machin, was the one who would be throwing tea cups about. Mel would put the fear of God into you, and Ken would put his arm round you, if that was what you needed, and there was a mutual respect between them and for them from the players.

But although Norwich hadn't hesitated to give me my chance in the first-team, there is always a difficulty for local lads when the club is signing players for big fees, and having to pay them big wages to attract them. I was a local and was already there, so they put me on the second level of wages, never the top. And over the years I had to compete for my first-team place with midfield players like Andy Townsend and Micky Phelan, who they had paid money for.

After winning the Milk Cup, Norwich were relegated and I didn't get too many games in the second tier — although I did score the goal that gave us the title, at Stoke.

Then I had a really good season in 1986-87 when I played 41 times and we finished fifth in the top division — the highest the club had ever been at that time — and it was a really good time to be around the club.

I genuinely think we might have won the league that season, because away from home we were incredible. We lost fewer away games than the four who finished above us — Everton, Liverpool, Tottenham, and Arsenal. We only lost two at home, and that was fewer than anyone other than Everton, the Champions. But we drew 10 home games and all the other four drew a lot less than that. If we could have turned some of those draws into victories...

Anyway, that summer, I was selected to go with the England under-21s to a tournament in Toulon. The manager of the under-21s was Dave Sexton — not Mike Bassett, despite what happened.

We drew 0-0 with Turkey and the manager gave us a curfew. We had to be in our hotel by 11. Me and Robert Rosario, my Norwich teammate, obviously shared a room and we were sitting in it playing cards. We were joined by Mark Brennan and Jason Dozzell, both from Ipswich. Then Steve Sedgley of Spurs and a mad Geordie by the name of Paul Gascoigne came into our room too. Gazza, who was still a Newcastle player at that stage, had burst on to the scene at that tournament, playing really incredibly, and all the focus was on him.

Ok, so there were six of us in this one hotel room in Toulon. The hotel was near the marina, and the room looked out on all the amazing yachts and all the people out for the evening. Gazza was saying, 'Come on, let's go out. Come on.' And in the end we did. We just walked out in our England polo shirts and tracksuits. Of course, we just happened to see a little cocktail bar, and its lights were twinkling and it drew us in. A few Sambucas later we thought it was time to go back to the hotel, but Gazza and Sedge went off to get a kebab, so the other four of us strolled back without them.

So it's me, Rob, Jason and Mark going back to our hotel. In the marina were lots of little rowing boats tied up and Jason decided to jump from boat to boat, and we all knew nothing could possibly go wrong. How could it? But each time he jumped, the boat he landed in rocked wildly, and the water was getting more and more disturbed. But Jason wasn't at all disturbed — until, for some inexplicable reason, he misjudged one jump and went straight in the plonk. That was when he remembered that he couldn't swim.

And at the same time he realised how much he had recently spent on a new watch. So he was shouting, 'Save my watch,' and shoving his arm up in the air while he thrashed about, and we tried to grab any bit of him to stop him going under and then to haul him out.

He was soaked through, and we had all made a tiny little bit of noise. The hotel was only about 60 yards away and Dave Sexton had watched it all from the window of his room.

We trained the next morning and nothing was said. But in the afternoon there was a meeting and we were reprimanded for letting down our country. We took it all without a murmur — and certainly didn't let on that Gazza and Sedge had got away with breaking the curfew because they'd gone to find kebabs.

The team lost in the quarter-finals and when the next two under-21 squads were announced the East Anglian quartet — me, Rob, Jason and Mark — were all left out both times. Our non-selection wasn't explained publicly for a while, but then a Sunday newspaper revealed that we had been banned for nine months for our extra-curricula activity in Toulon. The paper printed pictures of the four of us, and superimposed bars in front of us as if we were in prison.

Gazza went from strength to strength with England, though, so I don't agree with all the people who say kebabs were bad for him!

I had played for my country at every level from schoolboy to under-21s, and the FA eventually forgave me enough to award me two England B caps. But I never got a full cap and I think that was because I went and played in Scotland. It was a weaker league up there, and if I had stayed at Norwich I believe I would have got a call up to the full England team. That is a regret I have.

But, back at Norwich after the England under-21 adventure, Ken Brown was sacked just a few months into the 1987-88 season, and Dave Stringer got the job.

As a player, Dave had experienced the same situation as me — being a local lad competing with big name signings. I think you have to work harder, or perhaps be better, to win everyone's respect in those circumstances. Dave had certainly done that as a player, and then he was youth team manager when Norwich won the FA Youth Cup in 1983.

But it was a big step when he followed Ken as manager and, being a local lad, he had the same situation again of being known by everyone instead of being someone who'd been sort of 'stolen' from another club.

As manager, he had Dave Williams working with him, and Dave W was the calm one whereas Dave S was the tense one because he wanted so much for his local football club to succeed. It meant so much to him and he was Norwich City through and through. He didn't want to let the club and people down.

Dave Stringer's first full season in charge was 1988-89. We went top in September, were still there until December, and were still on course for what would have been an incredible League and FA Cup double when we reached the FA Cup semi-final, in April. I played in the semi, against Everton at Villa Park, but we didn't have Robert Fleck because his father had died that week. We missed him massively, and it was a scrappy game, which we lost to a scrappy goal. A ball came over from our right and Ian Crook, facing his own goal, reached out a leg to stop it going past him but hit the ball against our bar. They got a shot from the rebound, which was blocked, but the ball rebounded again and Pat Nevin, a foot or so out, scuffed his shot but scored.

The other semi-final that day was the Liverpool-Forest game, which became the Hillsborough disaster, which put things in perspective for us. We'd only lost a football match. But it had an effect on us; we had six games left in the League, only won one of them, and finished fourth. The one League game we won in that run-in was a home game against Everton, but it didn't make up for losing to them in the semi. Finishing fourth meant we'd beaten the level set two seasons earlier, and had finished higher than any other Norwich team, but we were disappointed.

That season was the third time Norwich 'qualified' for Europe but were ruled out by the ban on English clubs. We should have earned a place in Europe by winning the Milk Cup in 1985 and for our league positions in 1987 and 1989.

But I did win Player Of The Season for Norwich in 1989 and that is something I look back on with pride.

The 1989-90 season didn't go so well for the team and the following November, 1991, I left Norwich for Glasgow Rangers. They were a massive club at that time, and they looked at me six times before making a move for me, but then they sold Mark Walters to Liverpool and needed a replacement.

So then I knew the move was on but Norwich had a home game against Forest and I was up against Stuart Pearce again. After two minutes I swapped wings and Dave Stringer asked me what I was doing. I didn't want to get kicked up in the air and end up in hospital instead of on my way to Glasgow, and Dave was probably the only person who didn't know.

In fact I didn't go to Glasgow after the game. I had to wait until the following day. Robert Chase, the Norwich chairman, wanted £1.5 million for me and Rangers had offered £1.2 million. In the end they shook hands on £1.25 million. I left with a bit of a heavy heart, because I'd signed a new, four-year contract with Norwich that year but I had people like Robert Fleck and Andy Townsend telling me that I wouldn't understand or believe how big a club Rangers were until I started playing for them.

So the only real doubt in my mind about joining them was that I would hamper my chances of playing for England. It seemed the right step for Dale Gordon, though, and I immediately knew the difference. At Norwich, if I was interviewed by the press, there'd be one or two of them and I would be wearing a dodgy shell-suit. When I did my press conference in Glasgow for my signing, it was in a special room, there were at least 30 media people there, and I had to be in shirt and tie.

The reason we had been successful at Norwich was that we had no stars. Or, rather, none of us regarded ourselves as superstars. But when I walked into the changing room at Ibrox, every peg was taken by someone with a huge reputation: Mark Hateley, Ally McCoist... guys like that. And of course, for me, I was no longer the local lad. I was someone they had paid good money for.

On my debut, against Dunfermline, I scored two, had one disallowed, and set up two, so I had set myself a high standard. But it continued to go well and I have the medals to show for it. I won the title twice up there, plus the Scottish Cup and the League Cup.

And, at last, I had the unbelievable experience of playing in the European Cup — the competition that was to become the Champions League. The ban on English clubs was lifted in 1992, and that year I played in one of the biggest matches Rangers have ever played: the 'Battle of Britain' against Leeds. Walter Smith, the Rangers manager, had introduced team rotation and I didn't play in the home leg — but I got my turn in the second leg at Elland Road. Away supporters were banned because the police feared trouble, but there was an incredible atmosphere. Eric Cantona came on for them as a sub, but we repeated the score from the first leg and won 2-1.

Oh, and I played in five 'Old Firm' derbies against Celtic and never lost. In fact I only played in one defeat at all in my two years at Rangers. So I should have stayed with them. But I wasn't selected for the 1992 Cup Final and that cheesed me off. Then West Ham came in for me during the summer and I remembered how much I had enjoyed playing against them for Norwich. Chadwell Heath, where West Ham train, was only a couple of hours by road from Norwich because the roads were getting better, and I had family reasons for moving back to England. It wasn't too long since my son, Remi, had been born. Harry Redknapp offered me better terms at West Ham than I was on in Glasgow, and so I decided to make the move.

I played about seven games for West Ham and then picked up a straightforward injury to my left knee and had a routine cartilage operation. But, because I was a £1 million signing, I felt under pressure to get fit quickly and I kept trying it too soon. Every time I tried to get training again, I kept breaking down and the injury escalated so that I had two more operations. I was never the same and in three years I only made 11 appearances.

They loaned me out to Peterborough and to Millwall, and eventually I went to Bournemouth, where I met up with Mel Machin again. I went there as his first-team coach, but the club were in terrible financial trouble, and things were so bad that one day someone working for the receivers jumped in my club car and drove it away.

I loved the coaching part of my six months in Bournemouth, and so I went home to the Great Yarmouth area and set up an academy. I managed Great Yarmouth and then Gorleston, where I got Robert Fleck to play for me. I ran an academy for Ipswich (sorry!) in Lowestoft and had a bar in Yarmouth, and then in 2013 the opportunity came to work in Dubai, in the sun.

I joined a football coaching company in Dubai as director of football and was with them for about three years. Then I had to have a hip replacement — as you do! It was my left hip. I think all the years of playing and training took their toll. And I still run a lot. I'm out running all the time and I think it all caught up with me — which is something not many could do when I was a bit younger!

Or perhaps jumping off too many tables after nice lunches. Either way, the old hip was really messed up; one bone was grinding against another and it got to a point when it was too uncomfortable.

In 2016, I joined a radio station called *Dubai Eye*. When Euro 2016 was on in France, I was the station's voice of the tournament and thoroughly enjoyed it. We were based at the Jumeirah Beach Hotel, which is one of the famous Dubai landmarks, and I've been with *Dubai Eye* ever since. I do a Monday night show on football and contribute to other shows during the week.

In September 2016, I got back to coaching as well. I set up my own club DG Pro FC. It's a youth football club for children aged seven to 12. It's gone really, really well, and in 2017 the under-11s won the league and cup double. I have kids from all over: Egyptians, Russians, French, Danes, Hungarians, Slovakians. My philosophy for youth football is, first and foremost, to let the kids enjoy themselves and learn from making mistakes. I know the game has moved on from when I played but I think that when kids go to pro clubs too many of them become regimented. The spark they had that caused them to get noticed is drilled out of them.

That wasn't what happened to me, and I am very grateful for that. These days it feels as if I've come a long way, in every sense, from Caister, and I have certainly done a lot of things since leaving Norwich City — in the game at Rangers in Scotland, for instance, and outside the game since retiring. But I think of Norwich as the place and the club where I was given the opportunity. I had some great teammates too.

My biggest regret was getting injured almost as soon as I joined West Ham from Rangers in 1993. I was 26, with so much more to offer and with the way the game was going — with all the razzamatazz of Sky and the Premier League — it was precisely the wrong time to get crocked. It was a blow in another way too. When I left Carrow Road after that final game, against Forest, I felt as if I had unfinished business at Norwich and might go back some day. That just didn't happen though. The injury made that impossible.

Dale Gordon grew up in Caister, scored 43 goals in 248 games for Norwich, was player of the season in 1989, and was voted into the club's Hall Of Fame in 2002, 11 years after he left in a £1.2 million transfer to Glasgow Rangers. He later managed both Gorleston and Yarmouth, and now lives and works in Dubai.

10

He had to follow one critical season with the help of three-week old *Pink Uns* while behind the razor wire of a military compound in Afghanistan. These days **Tom Smith** is rather better informed about Norwich City. He is the newest member of the club's board and, by some distance, the youngest. On his appointment as a director, he promptly set about meeting supporters — as many as he could at every opportunity. This Tale is the chance for fans to get to know him.

LONGING AND BELONGING

A confession: I almost supported a team that plays in blue and white. Ugh. Born in 1981, I grew up in South London with my non-football-supporting mum and sister, and it might as well have been a million miles away from Carrow Road. My parents were divorced, and anyway my dad thought that rugby was the only game to which it was worth paying attention. So I didn't have a strong force pulling me towards football at first. The first time I ever saw a live match was watching Palace as part of a school outing (I don't remember the opposition, but I do remember thinking Selhurst was a bit shabby even then…). But the other local team, Millwall, were the superior of the two in 1988-89, having won promotion to the top division the season before.

One of my best friends, David, was a huge Lions fan, as was his dad. Their end of terrace house up the road from ours was painted white with royal blue window frames and drainpipes in homage to their team. David's dad had even ingeniously contrived to be named Dennis, or Den for short. And so, blissfully unaware of the hooliganism issue in late-80s football (not least at Cold Blow Lane), I went to a couple of matches in deepest Bermondsey with David and Den.

Whether my family were at all concerned by me going to Millwall I'm not sure. But I do know that before long Delia and Michael (Wynn Jones), my paternal aunt and uncle, offered to take me to watch Millwall play their team — Norwich City — at the Den. I don't blame them if they felt that I could do better than following my local team. It was January 1989. I'd just had my eighth birthday and I remember little about the match first-hand, only later learning that it was an absolute classic. Goals from Ian Butterworth and Mark Bowen saw Norwich take an early lead before being pegged back to 2-2 before half time. In the second half, a magnificent display of keeping by Bryan Gunn kept City in the game, before a stunning 90th-minute winner by Robert Fleck took all three points. What a match! A grainy YouTube video of the encounter — it was the first game televised live from the Den — has filled in some of the blanks, but I wish I could remember more.

So that was my first City game, and it proved to be a beautifully timed intervention by Delia and Michael. The team did their bit to win me over too: Norwich were flying high at the time, finishing the season fourth ahead of Millwall in tenth, with Manchester United (who?) down in eleventh. Successive seasons in the top division followed. Like many other fans of my generation, I assumed that this, of course, was the natural order of things. And even if a scintilla of doubt about my allegiance had remained (it didn't — I became known at school as the oddball kid who supported an unusual team) along came the UEFA Cup run to confirm my faith. Sitting on the floor at home in London in 1993, my nose inches from our ancient TV as my team — my team! — beat the exotic-sounding Bayern Munich, any thoughts of Millwall were far behind me. Becoming a Norwich fan was the second-best decision I have ever made. And, let's be honest, it was inevitable wasn't it?

Of course, what I was too young to realise at the time was that underneath that success on the pitch was the cavalier assumption that the new-found Premier League money would simply keep flowing. And we all know what happened next. Anyone who wants to understand just how close the club came to disappearing in the mid-90s need only to read Michael's chapter in *Tales From The City* volume one. If you haven't, I recommend it.

Since I joined the club's board in January 2015, a question I'm regularly asked is, 'what was it like growing up with Delia and Michael?' I tend to gently point out that this does a significant disservice to my mum, who showed remarkable dedication, and not a small amount of patience, raising my sister and me. I can only say that having Delia and Michael's love and support was an enormous privilege. As kids, my sister and I would regularly stay with them at their cottage in Suffolk, and I will always be grateful to them for remaining in my life after my parents split. But I'm not sure that our relationship would make a TV series worth viewing: each episode would just be us watching football, talking football, eating too much, and then falling asleep in front of the television (Sky Sports, naturally). Suffice to say that we share two great loves — Norwich City and food — and are very close.

My earliest visits to Carrow Road in the late 80s and early 90s were on occasions when Delia or, most likely, Michael would take me when school and travel allowed. They weren't directors then but had two season tickets in the City Stand. In general, I have a terrible memory for individual games, goal-scorers' names and so on, so the games themselves are rather a blur. One was certainly the 3-1 home defeat by Manchester United in April 1993 when we were going for the title — we arrived late because of traffic just in time to hear Ryan Giggs score the first while we were still outside on Carrow Road.

But my strongest memories are actually of the strangeness, the newness, of the experience. Not just football but Norfolk — a place I now love and call home. The walk to the ground from the County Hall car park, where Michael had charmed one of the attendants into reserving a grassy space for him

right next to the exit. The half-time biscuit scrimmage in the
County Lounge: a contest of determination, strategy, and skill,
where first prize was a biscuit with any kind of filling. (Could
I ever outwit the canny regulars? No chance. It's a carve-up.)
The unrecognisable businesses, for a boy from Forest Hill,
who advertised on the South Stand hoardings: Fitt Signs. Pilch.
Beeline Taxis. If I ever have space for a dedicated football
room at home, the sofa will come from Hellesdon Leather
Furniture. And from later years I remember the hoardings
around the former Boulton and Paul site, crudely daubed with
two memorable words: Chase Out.

I continued to travel to Carrow Road with Delia and Michael
throughout my years at school. I was about 15 when they first
told me that they had accepted an offer to join the club's board.
That preceded the share issue that left them, once the dust had
settled, with a majority holding. The chronology of events is
covered in Michael's own Tale and I was just a spectator, so
I'll skip the details. I'll just reflect that at that age I certainly
didn't understand much about share issues or the finer points
of corporate governance; I don't think I had ever considered
the strange fact that football clubs were commodities to be
bought and sold. Nor did I conceive of the scale of the task
they had taken on: untangling onerous contracts left over from
the previous regime, servicing the mountain of debt, urgently
looking for new revenue and sources of capital. And all the
while trying to focus on the two most important ingredients:
the football and the fans.

But I remember one thing: I remember why they did it. I
recall that clearly because they told me at the time, and because
we've had many conversations since. It was not an investment
or a business opportunity. As Delia has regularly told me, and
as most club owners will affirm (with the possible exception of
the Glazers at Manchester United), you might as well pile your

cash up on the pitch and set fire to it. Nor was it an ego-boost or a retirement hobby; having responsibility for a football club isn't exactly a cruise in the Med. They did it simply because the club was in trouble and they felt that they could help. They wanted to preserve an institution that had brought them joy. They recognised that a thriving community should have a football club at its heart. And for the club itself to thrive, to serve its community, it needed at the very least to exist.

After leaving school in London I headed north to attend university in Liverpool. Norwich was five hours away, but I would regularly return to Carrow Road whenever my studies and travel allowed. Luckily the North West is one of the most densely populated footballing landscapes in the world, and so I made plenty of away games; and I slowly started racking up a healthy list of grounds visited — a list that now numbers somewhere in the low 90s. But when I wasn't there, it was painful. It makes me feel depressingly old to remember that at the start of the millennium the Internet wasn't available on your phone. It was tethered firmly to a desk at the university library, and someone else was always using it. Roy Waller's Radio Norfolk exclamations were lost in static. For the committed fan without a reliable dial-up connection, let alone broadband, fingernails were bitten to the quick while watching the tortuous teletext page-flip. That was how I experienced much of the 2001-02 play-offs season. Nothing would have stopped me from attending the play-offs themselves, though. The final, in Cardiff, was an experience like no other, but for the rest of my life I will remember the semi-final second leg and our glorious 1-0 defeat (our best ever?) at Molineux. I somehow contrived to acquire an empty champagne bottle, which was full when Sky gave it to the players, which loudly proclaims, 'We're going to Cardiff.' Wolves had let themselves down, again... but only because they were playing a superior team.

As years passed and I left Liverpool, I started work for the Ministry of Defence in a role that saw me living for periods in Bristol, Derby, Rugby, Poole, and London. But Norwich was the place that I kept coming back to, drawn by family and the inevitability of the next fixture. So in 2007, wanting to get on the property ladder, I finally put down roots in Norwich and bought a flat near the club, where I still live today. Almost 20 years since Delia and Michael had first taken me to Carrow Road, I had fallen in love with a city that is cool, compact, friendly, and situated minutes from some of England's most stunning countryside. After South London and Liverpool, it was refreshing, and it's now definitively home.

I suppose it was inevitable that my newfound status as a Norwich resident would coincide with a pretty dismal period as far as football was concerned. The story of our relegation to the third tier and the opening day of the next season against Colchester doesn't need re-telling — and having been at both The Valley and Carrow Road for those two awful events, I don't much fancy re-living the nausea I felt at the time.

But, like many others, I found great enjoyment and drew some valuable lessons from our season in League One. For all the money, glitz, and glamour in the Premier League (and to a lesser extent in the Championship), I think that the true heart of British football exists somewhere deep within that enormous, colourful, vibrant pyramid of smaller clubs further down the hierarchy, and with the army of dedicated individuals who keep them alive. It's far from an absolute rule, but there seems to be an indefinable closeness, a rapport between clubs, staff, players, and fans in the lower leagues, which diminishes as money, fame, and stadium size increase. There is a unity of purpose, often in the face of adversity, which can generate a sense of belonging, a pride, a spirit, and a commitment worth many millions on the wage bill. Witness Sutton and Lincoln's achievements in the 2016-17 FA Cup and tell me otherwise.

As the lucky recipient of several dozen wildly varying versions of boardroom hospitality on match days up and down the leagues, I can also attest to the generally inverse relationship between a club's league position and the warmth of the welcome. There are honourable exceptions of course, but do I prefer the Pirelli Stadium or Stamford Bridge? I know where I'd go if I wanted to meet real football people. Does that mean I would be happier if Norwich kept League One company more regularly? Emphatically not! The big-business clubs may sometimes lack soul, but a City win at Stamford Bridge means so much, and it would be absurd to claim that doesn't matter. We must, must, must have the ambition to compete at the very pinnacle of the sport, to reach our full potential, otherwise we might as well just pack up and go home. But do I think we ought to learn from our time in League One? Ought we to recognise that the most valuable lessons might be the ones where the solution isn't simply more cash? Emphatically yes.

After a tumultuous August and a stuttering September, Norwich started to get into their stride in League One in October 2009, winning four games out of five. Our resurgence gathered pace in November and December, only slightly dented by a couple of draws and the traditional early FA Cup exit away at Carlisle. For me personally, the 2-0 home victory against Millwall (for whom I still retain a soft spot) in December was almost the last I would see of our League One adventure in the flesh. The Ministry of Defence decided that I had visited enough provincial towns and cities for a while, and that my next stop would be a few months in southern Afghanistan, where a US troop surge had generated fresh impetus in the fight against the Taliban.

There were more civvies like me out in Afghanistan than
people probably imagine — working in a huge variety of
diplomatic, advisory or logistical roles. The only thing we had
in common was that we were universally treated like wayward
children by those in uniform — unable to cross a road unaided,
a kindly pat on the head never too far away. My job was to act
as advisor to the British commanding officer and bridge the
gap to my team back at home. Barricaded for the majority of
the time behind high walls and razor wire for up to six months,
it was pretty safe — no comparison at all to what our troops
faced out in the green zone. But 18-hour days were the norm,
home was a corner of a dusty room shared with three other
army officers, weekends consisted of an extra hour in bed on
Fridays, and Internet access was strictly rationed. Worst of all,
Defence personnel like me were subject to military regulations,
meaning that alcohol was strictly forbidden. Our Foreign Office
colleagues had a more civilised outlook on life!

For anyone so detached from home the real highlight each
week was the mailbag. And I had more reason to long for its
arrival more keenly than most… match highlights. I usually
managed to find our results more or less on the day of the
game, but I will forever be grateful to Val Lemmon, long-time
PA to the manager at Norwich (now retired), who faithfully
copied DVDs of all the matches. Delia then queued at the Post
Office in Stowmarket to send them out me via the BFPO, along
with copies of the *Pink Un*. The parcels were anything up to
three weeks late, but on a base where a six-month-old copy
of *Loaded* magazine counted as quality literature, they were like
manna from heaven. That was how I watched Paul Lambert
inspire our audacious 0-5 revenge against Colchester: the
moment when I was sure that we'd go straight back up.

Against the odds I managed to arrange my R&R for April,
so that I was back at The Valley when my confidence was

finally vindicated and we were promoted straight back to the Championship. With a pleasing circularity it was in the same corner of South East London where we'd left it. The end-of-season celebrations were too late for me and I was back in Afghanistan, albeit with a slight change of scenery as I was posted up to the international HQ in Kabul for a further few months. But I couldn't have been happier than to have been at Charlton on that day when our Championship return was sealed to savour the moment with Delia and Michael. I count myself very lucky to have shared moments like that with the people closest to me, and I'm very grateful to the football club for writing the script.

One of the most special moments in my life was when my half-sister Rose and her family visited Norwich from their home in New Zealand in January 2017. It was the first time I had met my nine-month-old nephew Flynn, and his attendance at a game was non-negotiable. Football has always been a family occasion for us. My grandmother, Etty, is 97 years young and attends every home game as well as every under-23 match at Carrow Road. She has been an enormous influence on my life, and watching our young players somehow seems to restore a bit of her own youthfulness too. So at the 2-2 FA Cup draw in January 2017 against Southampton there were four generations of my family watching on: from a nine-month-old debutant to a 97-year veteran. I'm pleased to say that Flynn loved what I hope will be the first match of many... and I'll do my best to dissuade him from supporting Millwall.

Change is an inevitability in families, in life and in business: sometimes you seek it, sometimes it comes out of nowhere. But it seemed that change was everywhere at Norwich in that League One season. Looking back now it feels like a regeneration, because of how much the club changed between August and May. That it happened at all was due to the unshakeable focus and tireless efforts of chief executive David McNally and everyone at Carrow Road, while behind the scenes the board, led by Alan Bowkett, worked wonders to provide the financial breathing room the club needed. But one other factor helped enormously: week in, week out, our amazing fans would pack out Carrow Road and away ends around the country. That unceasing support gave the team the belief it needed to win game after game, and it also gave our creditors confidence that the club had the financial sustainability to recover. If ever there was proof of the power of supporters to push their club forwards, of togetherness and positivity making a real difference both on and off the pitch, this was it. If we as a club could capture that sensation and unleash it every season there would be no limit to our achievements. But we all know it's more complicated than that.

I was back in the UK in time for the start of our first season back in the Championship in 2010, that incredible year defined by the image of a moustachioed Grant Holt smashing in a hat-trick against Ipswich. It was legendary. I made every game that year and the journey was magical, with a sublime crescendo in April as we beat Forest, Ipswich (what was the score again?), Derby (Chris Goreham's finest moment), and Portsmouth to secure second place. After our season-long loan to League One, that was as close to perfection as anyone could ask. The League trophy would have been the icing on the cake, but I didn't care.

And so City were back in the Premier League. After three away wins in January and February, we were almost safe by April 2011 when I was off to the other side of the world again, this time with my partner Alice. She had been offered a posting in Canberra, Australia, while I found a position with the British High Commission. It was the kind of opportunity you seize when you are young, or never at all.

Alice had never been to a live football match before so I gently suggested that if we were going to travel to the other side of the world together, she really ought to understand more about the man she was going with. And that meant understanding his football team. So with the confidence of a true romantic, I drove Alice to Stoke in early March to witness a depressing 1-0 defeat in the most dispiriting, drizzly, Stoke-like atmosphere you can imagine. It was dreadful, illuminated by a single shining ray of sunlight: the debut of a recent signing from Leeds called Johnny Howson. Alice has adored him, probably slightly too much, ever since.

We ended up spending three years overseas. Technology had thankfully moved on to the point where video streaming meant that I could watch every league game live. As I write this in mid-2017, Carrow Road holds 27,244 people, but the @NorwichCityFC Twitter account has more than 480,000 followers and the club's Facebook page more than 800,000 likes. But it's trite merely to observe that modern technology provides more ways than ever before to connect with the club from afar, however true. The real challenge is to ensure that those technologies provide a useful service for fans and don't just become another marketing tool. Matches will be streamed live on more and more platforms but we need to ensure that they also provide a real opportunity to connect and converse meaningfully. But in Canberra, I was simply content not to be watching teletext again.

It was also in Australia that I became conscious of the network of overseas fans' groups that bring together Norwich fans from far and wide. The Canaries Down Under are one of the larger factions, with volunteers arranging regular meet-ups in Sydney, Melbourne, Brisbane, and Auckland. There's even an annual East Angliand Down Under, where the CDU play their Ipswich-supporting counterparts. Being stuck in

Canberra I sadly never made any of the meets. But I followed their activities regularly through social media and I saw how, even many thousands of miles away, being part of a club is a passport to friendship and opportunity. There are similar groups of supporters all around the world — including in the USA, Scandinavia, even Israel — and their presence provides comfort to Norfolk exiles and indigenous City fans alike. They add enormously to the vibrancy of the club.

In Canberra, Alice increasingly began to join me on the sofa for 2am kick-offs, watching on as I struggled to sync a decent video stream of City's action with Chris Goreham's outstanding commentary on Canaries World. (Incidentally, how Chris hasn't been snapped up by Radio 5 Live is a mystery to me. His ability to describe a game with accuracy and passion makes him worth a thousand Alan Greens.) And I was delighted that, three years later, I returned to the UK with Alice not just a confirmed City fan, but also my fiancée. If supporting Norwich was the second-best decision I ever made, convincing Alice to marry me was the first. We got hitched in London in 2015, less than a month after that incredible day out at Wembley.

There are countless fans' groups in the UK too, of course, both for Norfolk-based supporters and domestic exiles. The breadth of opinion, experience and interests encompassed by those groups is vast and valuable. I've a particular fondness for the Capital Canaries, not just because they represent fans from my home town, but because they have the good sense to organise meetings in a Bermondsey brewery! The Northern Canaries are another group with a strong record of meeting in pubs... although the 2017 venue was atop a small mountain in Sheffield, the climb to which almost left us looking for a new MD. I empathise with the aims of the Barclay End Norwich, whose mission is find ways of generating a fearsome atmosphere at Carrow Road, and who are vocal supporters of the introduction of safe standing areas — an issue on which a broader debate is clearly due. And I have nothing but praise for the efforts of the Proud Canaries, led by the inspirational Di Cunningham, to highlight the challenges faced by the LGBT community in our sport. Football should be for everyone, regardless of ethnicity, gender or sexual orientation. I'm proud not only that Norfolk is a tolerant and welcoming society, but also that the Proud Canaries are in the forefront of the national conversation on the issue.

I recognise that I've had an extremely privileged relationship with the club over the years, thanks to nothing more than a simple accident of birth. And over the years I have had the pleasure of getting to know far more committed supporters than me, fans who are determined to watch every match live regardless of cost, distance or inconvenience, fans like my friend Debs, who hasn't missed a competitive game home or away since 1983. She is not alone in that achievement, and the dedication of fans like her is nothing short of remarkable. But if my times away from Norwich have taught me anything, it's that your passion for a team isn't always measured by your proximity to its stadium, how many live games you see or where you sit in the ground. Having an allegiance to a club is more than that — it's about being part of a tight-knit community and supporting it in whichever way your life permits. It's about sharing an identity that you can use anywhere on the planet.

I suppose the broader lesson is that supporting a football club is more than a pastime for many of us; it's an integral, visceral part of our lives. Without it, a piece of us is missing. Sometimes life gets in the way, it's inconvenient, sure. But in simple terms it's a sense of belonging. Belonging to something that is bigger than all of us, something on which we can pin our hopes. Somewhere we can celebrate our successes or drown our sorrows. Something that will outlast us. Something we can be proud of. It's a deeply comforting sensation. To anyone who has ever said, 'It's just a game'… you have no idea what you're missing.

I never had any expectation that Delia and Michael would ask me to join the board of directors. I know better than most how deeply they care for the football club and for all the people who work for it. And I know better than anyone how desperate they are to see it succeed in years to come. It is a huge honour for me to know that they trust me to have a small hand in shaping the club's future.

When they asked me in January 2016, I didn't find it too much of a culture shock. I already knew a significant number of the senior staff and all the existing directors well because we attended matches together each week. There were no nasty surprises on the business front either, not just because the club is widely recognised in the game as being sensibly and transparently run, but because Delia, Michael and I have talked about little else for years. But I didn't entirely foresee that the following 18 months would be quite so eventful, with a number of high-profile changes at the top of the club generating endless column-inches as we looked to find the right 'fit' for a club that had almost tripled in size since the League One days. In the midst of all that we suffered relegation, endured a disappointing season back in the Championship, appointed a new head coach and faced a host of other small challenges. Not exactly the year any of us hoped for, but certainly never a dull moment.

So what have been my impressions since becoming a director? Firstly, I've enjoyed being able to spend more time getting to know a group of individuals who rarely make headlines or attract praise, but who really make the club what it is: our staff. Norwich City is a complex organisation that employs around 300 people full-time at Carrow Road and

Colney, plus many more on a part-time or casual basis. I have found them to be dedicated, professional, considerate, and extremely hard-working. More to the point, they are almost all City fans too, and they care as much about the club as anybody. They deserve our enthusiastic support for their efforts and our wholehearted recognition for their achievements.

I have also spent a significant amount of time getting to know the Community Sports Foundation, the club's official charity. I admit that I didn't fully realise that our club, through 25 years of hard work, has built one of the largest football club charitable foundations in the country. CSF's 80-strong team, supported by a small army of part-time coaches and volunteers, help more than 38,000 individuals every year, through sports, health, education and enterprise programmes. Our CSF spends significantly more on charitable causes than its counterparts at Manchester United and Liverpool. None of its funding is drawn from the football club or the playing budget. It's a remarkable organisation that uses the power of sport to inspire and support people to reach their own goals in life. It represents the very best of our club and our community, and I take huge pride in my role as one of its trustees. I could write a whole book talking about their inestimable value to the club, and to the people of Norwich and Norfolk. Perhaps one day I will. But for now I will simply say this: we should all be very proud of the work that the CSF team do and the outcomes they achieve.

But more than anything, through both the club and CSF, I've had the opportunity to meet more of my fellow City fans than ever before. It's been a huge privilege. In particular I've appreciated the invitations I have received to the Norwich City Fans Social Club, which organises a range of social events of City fans regardless of age, gender or opinion. Diane Blazer and her dedicated team of volunteers work tirelessly to make these events happen. They are enormous fun and I'm delighted that the club has supported them from the outset.

Since I first started watching Norwich City, football has changed beyond recognition — for both better and worse. The money flowing through the game has increased exponentially even though, for many clubs, it remains a slippery commodity to grasp. The financial chasm between the top clubs and the rest has widened dramatically, and as I write, the big six clubs are pushing for an even larger slice of the pie. Demographics are changing too: stadia have become more family-friendly than ever, even as the average age of fans has steadily increased. The days when women were something to be tolerated, not welcomed, has passed, and other inequalities have begun to be addressed. And while the litany of clubs entering administration or disappearing altogether in the last decade has sharpened attention on the governance of our national game, little of substance has been done to prevent financial crises from happening again and again.

Throughout all this I've sat round countless dinner tables with Delia and Michael and we've chewed the fat. The most valuable lesson that they have taught me remains as true now as it was when they joined the board themselves: football is about people. Listen to them, value them, help them succeed. And as I have been on my own journey as a City fan, following from the stands at Carrow Road or from a grainy computer screen on the other side of the world, it has been the people I have encountered who have developed my understanding of what this incredible football club is about. It is my family, my friends, Alice, the dedicated staff at the club and the Foundation, and the thousands of supporters and followers at home and far away who have defined what this club means to me. It is they who make me almost burst with pride when I call myself a Norwich City fan.

If you asked me to state the things I want most from our football club they would be these: I want it to exist, so that I can belong. I want it to be successful, so that I can celebrate. I want it to play a positive role in its community, so that it brings people together and helps us all to grow. And I am aware of the irony of the following statement, coming as it does at the end of 5,000 self-indulgent words about myself: it's not about me, or you, it's about all of us. We all come from different backgrounds but football is what brings us together. And it is together that we are at our strongest. We must cherish that, respect each other, and be proud of the fine identity that we all share.

Tom Smith grew up in London and, later, his work for the Ministry of Defence took him around the country and across the globe. But he chose to make his home in Norwich because of the pull of Carrow Road, and joined the Norwich City board in 2015.

11

Gary Doherty played for Norwich during tumultuous times. He was the last signing of the transfer window as the club began life in the Premier League under Nigel Worthington and was still there, three managers later, when they slipped into the third tier. The next manager along, Paul Lambert, wanted him out of the door — but 'The Doc' had other ideas.

THE CASE FOR THE DEFENCE

BY GARY DOHERTY

I learned a work ethic at Norwich. And I am proud how I responded to major setbacks while I was at the club.

There were definitely some of those. The worst feeling for me personally was after the 7-1 defeat at home to Colchester at the start of the 2009-10 season in League One.

I know it was horrific for the fans, but at least they could go to the pub with their mates and talk about how useless the players were. But as a single guy, I went home and didn't even turn the lights on. I just sat in my flat in darkness. I put the TV on but it was on Sky Sports News, and when the scores from our division came up they had the word 'seven' written alongside the number 7, in case people didn't believe it. So I turned the telly off and sat there in silence and darkness. I had never experienced anything like that, at any level, not even as a kid.

We had signed Grant Holt during the summer, and he was so good in pre-season that I'd told all my mates we were going to have a brilliant season. They all came to the Colchester game, saw us lose 7-1 and were like, 'What were you on about?!'

We had a League Cup tie at Yeovil scheduled for the Tuesday, followed by a League game at Exeter on the Saturday, so we were booked into a hotel in the West Country for the week — and I was grateful to escape out of Norwich, away from all the local media and the supporters.

We won 4-0 at Yeovil, which lifted us a bit. But then Bryan Gunn was sacked as manager on the Thursday, before the Exeter match. The following midweek, on our way to play at Brentford, we learned that Paul Lambert was going to be manager. I knew all about Lambert's playing career, because I was a Celtic fan so I knew what he'd done with them. And I knew how he'd won the Champions League with Borussia Dortmund. I also knew his Colchester team had just ruined us.

When we started to win games under Paul, with Holty scoring goals, my mates were all like, 'You were right!' But, for me, Lambert's arrival brought a real tough challenge. I'd been captain under Gunny. But Lambert dropped me completely out of the picture straight away. He sat us all down and asked us what we thought had been wrong with us as a team, and he made a point of asking my opinion — so I thought for a moment, 'Perhaps he thinks I can contribute.' But as soon as we went out and started working on team shape, I wasn't involved and so I knew I wouldn't be picked for his first game — at home to Wycombe, which we won 5-2.

Next we had a League Cup game, at home to Premier League Sunderland. He made changes, and I got a game. But I didn't play well, we lost 4-1 and Lambert tore strips off me in the changing room afterwards. I thought, 'My days are numbered here.'

He called me into his office the next day and said, 'Look, I want you out of the door.' I'd been there six years by then, been relegated twice, and he wanted to change things. It wasn't a nice conversation to be in, but I thought it was fair enough that he was being straight with me.

A few clubs got in touch. But I had learned from my Tottenham days that football can change very quickly. I didn't want to quit Norwich and I thought, 'I'll stay put and see what happens for a while at least.'

We only won one of the next five League One matches. I say, 'we', but I wasn't involved at all. Me and a few others, including Wes, had been told to train with the youth team. The manager actually went public and told the local Press that I didn't figure in his plans at all. But I look back with some pride, because I continued to work hard, alongside the kids, and tried to be professional.

Then, before a Tuesday night home game against Orient, he called me into his office and said, 'Look, I'm not coming cap in hand to you, but I would like you to play in this game. I'll understand, though, if you don't want to in the circumstances here, where you might be leaving.'

I said, 'I want to play.'

We smashed Orient. Wes had got back in the team a couple of games earlier and the manager kept me and him in the side for the rest of the season. And we started winning game after game. By the turn of the year we were in the top two, and when we went to Colchester and won 5-0 he said to me, in front of all the lads, 'I must have been out of my mind to drop you.' A lot of managers would not have been big enough to say that.

That game at Colchester was redemption for us. The pitch was unbelievably bad, but we'd had a few injuries and so Colchester were adamant for the game to go ahead, to play us when we might be weakened. Plus they thought Wes, who was playing out of his skin for us by then, would struggle in the mud, so I said to Wes, 'They think you can't play on this pitch.' In the first five minutes Wes made a crunching tackle — which wasn't his forte! — and I thought, 'OK, we are going to smash them.'

Fraser Forster — one of Lambert's best ever signings — made a key save at 0-0 and then we went on to settle scores from that 7-1. I got one of the goals — left foot, top corner — which was nice, and put some of my own demons to bed.

There were some good teams in that division. Leeds had good players, for instance, and at the start of the season I was thinking, 'If we can reach the play-offs we'll have done well.' But Lambert was always saying, 'We will win this division.' And at times, with Holty and Chrissy Martin up front and Wes just behind them, we were unstoppable. It was so enjoyable to play in that team.

Michael Nelson and me formed a good partnership in the middle of the defence, and with Fraser behind us we fancied we could hold out against anyone. And even if as a team we were on the ropes a bit, I thought that, if we could keep the opposition out, the manager would do something clever. I used to think, 'He will make a clever substitution, or switch the formation around a bit, and we will win.' We got so many late wins like that.

We clinched promotion with a 1-0 win at Charlton, which was another sort of redemption because that was where we'd been relegated the previous season. Then we won the next two games without conceding a goal, so we won the division and had recorded three consecutive clean sheets.

Holty picked up an injury and so I was captain for the final game of the season, at home to Carlisle. Someone told me that four consecutive clean sheets would be some sort of club record, so in the huddle on the pitch before the game I was all, 'Come on, lads. It will be great to keep another clean sheet.' So we conceded a goal in the first minute and another after about seven minutes!

We ended up losing 2-0, but it just didn't matter at all because we'd had a magnificent season that gave the whole club and the supporters some pride back. The supporters had been amazing too though. Some of the clubs we played had never seen such big crowds as we brought.

It was a proper competition, and we'd had such a bad start, but we won it. It was my favourite season of my whole career, and gave me the only League medal I have.

By then, I was established and settled as a centre-back, and I really wish someone had told me it was my best position when I was quite young. But some people thought I was best as a striker.

There were times that I played for Tottenham on the Saturday at centre-half in the Premier League, and then I'd go and join the Irish team for a midweek game and have to be an international striker. You need to work hard and learn to play in the Premier League. There are different things to learn as an international player. But I was having to try to learn two positions as well.

Glenn Hoddle said to me at Tottenham that I could use playing as a centre-half to help me become a better striker, and vice versa. But I didn't think like that. All I had were quite negative thoughts. I'd think, 'A good centre-half plays in that position for his whole life, but I'm not being allowed to do that.'

I know that Dion Dublin says in this book that when he played at centre-back, he benefitted by knowing what the striker was going to do. But he was a striker who played some games in defence late in his career. In my case, I was a young, developing player who wasn't allowed to concentrate on learning one set of skills and knowledge.

As a kid, I was a striker. The first time I kicked a football was when I started playing for an under-9s team in Luton, the town I'd moved to when I was six.

I was born in Donegal. I remember falling off my bike outside our house there, but that is probably my only memory of living in Ireland.

I got taken on by Luton quite young. The youth team manager was John Moore, who was a really tough Scottish guy who taught me good values. Luton's youth team were really successful. We got to the semi-finals of the FA Youth Cup and four or five have gone on to play in the Premier League.

I was probably playing more games at centre-half by then, but in the Youth Cup run I played up front and I made my first-team debut up front as well at 17 against Millwall. It was a really big match for Luton, because Millwall had a history of violent fan trouble when they played at Kenilworth Road. So it was a big moment for me when the manager, Lennie Lawrence, sent me on for the last 20 minutes up front.

Alongside my progression to the first-team at Luton, I was playing a lot of international youth football for Ireland. I went to the 1997 UEFA European Under-18 Championship finals in Iceland and scored against France. The following year that championship was held in Cyprus, and we won it. We beat Germany on penalties in the final.

Then in 1999 I was in the Republic squad that reached the round of 16 in the world under-20 championships in Nigeria. That time we lost on penalties, though, to the hosts.

So things were going well for me, and I knew there were teams looking at me at Luton. George Graham was the Spurs manager and I heard he'd been at a couple of our games. Tottenham's director of football was David Pleat, the ex-Luton manager, and he was at loads of our games. So I sort of knew for some time that Spurs were one of the teams interested in me.

Luton still used me a lot in defence, but I scored in five consecutive games. The record was six, and I was going for that record against Gillingham on the Saturday. So I was a bit gutted when I got sold to Spurs on the Thursday! It was March 2000. They paid £1 million for me.

I made my Spurs debut at Old Trafford and that ground has so many big memories for me. I scored in an FA Cup semi-final against Arsenal there. I gave away a penalty there that led to a 1-0 defeat for Spurs and I made my two Premier League debuts there: for Tottenham and Norwich.

But after joining Spurs I spent four or five months in the reserves, playing my two different positions, before I got properly established. It was around January 2001 that I got into the first-team at centre-half and stayed there for the rest of that season. We had a fantastic FA Cup run and I scored in three rounds.

We lost to Arsenal in that Old Trafford semi-final, but I was finding the Premier League a lot easier than I had expected. It was going well. I was playing alongside Sol Campbell, and loved that.

He left in the summer, but I was still playing well and was established in the Premier League at centre-back. Then in the September I played in a League Cup game against Torquay. Glenn Hoddle was manager and he was going to rest me, but someone else got injured and so I played. Early in the first half I broke my left leg and ankle.

I've still got pins and plates in there. It was bad. I was out for the rest of the season. I try to look back on it positively, and say I would rather have broken my leg at Tottenham than a couple of years earlier at Luton. Tottenham were able to provide the very best medical help and the best rehab science. With all due respect to Luton, they just couldn't afford all that.

Spurs looked after me as well as any club at that time could have done, but it was a tough time for me, and the injury cost me a place in 2002 World Cup. I was a regular in the Ireland squad when the break happened and although I was playing again by the time the World Cup squad was announced — and had scored my first goal for Ireland — the selection came just too soon for me. Funnily enough, I thought it would help that I could play in two positions, but Mick McCarthy, the Ireland manager, rang me and said, 'You haven't played enough games so I've got to leave you out.'

So I missed out on the Japan and South Korea World Cup, which was tough to take. It was a blow. And, of course, what we know about nutrition has moved on. These days, if you break your leg, you know much more about getting your diet right during the recovery. I was just smashing back pasta, because we all thought it was what you were supposed to do. But I wasn't training at all, so I put on far too much weight. I blew up completely.

Once I was allowed to train, I worked really hard to get the weight off and get properly fit, but although I was still only 22, I had lost some of my pace. And, while I'd been out, Glenn had made a lot of his own signings. I always thought he believed I should be a striker. He picked me at centre-back, but he was always pushing me up front in training and talking to me about being a striker.

Glenn got sacked and Pleaty had a spell as manager. He liked me and I was back in the team as a regular and given a new five-year deal. But Pleaty's role was only as a caretaker manager, and Jacques Santini took over as manager, and my situation changed yet again.

I played all through the pre-season games ahead of the 2004-05 season. Then, Santini signed Noureddine Naybet, a Moroccan defender from Deportivo. Naybet was picked for the first game of the season. He was quite a bit older than me, and I could see what would happen. He would start games and me, the younger player, would be on the bench to come on for the last 20 minutes or so. So when Norwich came in for me, I was ready to go.

Norwich had just been promoted to the Premier League and their manager, Nigel Worthington, DEFINITELY wanted me as a centre-back. That swung it for me. I was 24: time to concentrate on one position. But then, second game of the season, we go to Old Trafford. I'm sitting on the bench, and Nigel turns to me and says, 'Do you think you've got a goal in you?' And he sent me on as a sub for my debut — to play up front. I went on for Matt Svenson.

The next match was away to Newcastle and Nigel kept me in the team — in attack. We went 2-0 down, but David Bentley pulled one back and then, with about 15 minutes to go, I hit the equaliser. So I couldn't complain about being in attack again.

I don't think I would have signed for Norwich if I'd known I was going to be switching roles quite a lot, but when I scored at Newcastle, and played really well, I thought, 'Oh, OK, maybe I can play up front for Norwich. They might have to play a bit more direct in the Premier League than Spurs do and maybe I can do well in attack.'

That was how I was. If I did all right, it made me think, 'Right, this is my position.' But if I played badly, it kind of gave me an excuse, which I am annoyed with myself for, looking back. If I had a bad game, or made a mistake, I'd say to myself, 'Well, I'm not really a centre-half.' Or, 'I'm not really a centre-forward.'

But, of course, Norwich were fighting to stay in the Premier League, and Nigel had to keep trying different things. There were times that season when we got taken apart. I remember we lost 4-1 in both matches against Arsenal, for instance, but for the majority of the season we held our own in games and we had some decent results. And signing Dean Ashton in the January was a game-changer. So was Youssef Safri when he established himself in the team. He could really tackle.

I got into the team, in defence, after about 15 games into the season, but towards the end of the season I knew I wasn't playing well. We lost 3-0 at Blackburn in the February — that was a miserable game — and I lost my place to Jason Shackell.

I think about that one season with Norwich in the Premier League and I know I wasn't in good enough shape. Where we were as a team, compared to some of the clubs who could spend lots more money on players, it meant that we had to work a lot harder as individuals and as a team. We needed to be intense but I wasn't fit enough.

By the time I was 30, and into the later stages of my career, I was a very good trainer. But at Norwich it took me too long to realise the work ethic that was needed. I am not proud about that.

In the dressing room after we were relegated at Fulham in the last game, nobody was talking. Before the match, the saying had been, 'It took a season of 46 games to get to the Premier League. Now we only have to get it right in one game to stay in the Premier League.' But that day at Fulham was a shocker.

I took stock of myself as a Norwich player that summer and am quite proud I did. It would have been easy to tell myself, 'I'm a Premier League player. I'm not cut out for the Championship. Someone will come in for me. I don't have to worry about Norwich.'

But that summer I was flat out, running every day, determined to get myself fit and have a right go with Norwich. I wanted to be fit enough to play for them — and to play for Nigel, who certainly expected a work ethic. I had an apartment in Trowse and I used to go and do laps that took in a bit of running by the river there. On other days I'd go into the training ground at Colney and do sprints and stuff on the pitches there. Usually I was the only one about. I worked really hard.

When we reported back for pre-season, Nigel saw how fit I was, and saw my attitude too. He was buzzing. So I started the season in the team, alongside Craig Fleming, ahead of Shack. That was a big turn-around, because I hadn't even been on the bench at Fulham at the end of the previous season.

We started the 2005-06 season at home to Coventry. Ash gave us the lead in the first half, and I was cruising along in top gear. But I probably didn't understand my new body because I completely ran out of gas. That was my first ever game in the Championship, and it is right when people say it is the most physically demanding division of them all. It hits you like a hammer. We ended up drawing 1-1 and Nigel told me, rightly, that my performance had dipped far too much in the later stages of the match.

So I was dropped again. I was left out for the next six matches. But I kept eating healthily and keeping myself strong and fit and, meanwhile, results didn't go well. We had played seven, won one, drawn three and lost three. So Nigel changed things again, and I was back — this time alongside Callum Davenport, who was on loan from Sours — for the derby against Ipswich at Portman Road. It was one of my best games for Norwich, I believe, and we won 1-0. I set up the goal — a nice long diagonal pass to Hucks.

I kept my place after that and won the fans' Player Of The Season. We were really disappointed that we didn't make the play-offs. We finished ninth and the supporters obviously expected more than we delivered, but from a personal point of view, I was proud of how I had got my act together. I can look back with pride and know that I proved something to myself and to Nigel.

But losing can become a habit, just like winning can. We'd spent the Premier League season having too many defeats and then we'd had a disappointing season back in the Championship under Nigel. The club had sold Ash in the January, and then, in the close season, Rob Green left and we'd lost a top, top goalkeeper.

In the second month of the following season, 2006-07, we had a really poor run of results, and Nigel was sacked at the start of October. Peter Grant came in. I liked him, and he picked me regularly, but he just couldn't reverse that losing momentum.

He lasted until the October of the 2007-08 season before he resigned. He signed some good players, but some of the lads he brought in from Scotland probably weren't able to adapt quickly enough to the Championship.

So in came Glenn Roeder. I have to say, again, that I liked him — because he liked me and did everything he could to help me get games. I had a lot of back issues at that time, and I had a triple hernia. I was going through the mill a bit, but Glenn structured my training so that I could keep playing.

He kept us up in 2007-08, which was an achievement. Then he signed Wes Hoolahan, Sammy Clingan, had Leroy Lita on loan and some young loan players like Ryan Bertrand for the 2008-09 season. Some were brought in quite late, so that they missed the pre-season and we didn't have much time to bond as a squad. And I remember wondering whether the young loan players would sink or swim if they were thrown into the Championship.

Glenn was sacked in January, Bryan Gunn took over, but we were relegated on the last day of the season — at Charlton. I played that day and it was an awful day for the fans and the whole club. Charlton were already relegated, so they relaxed. We were nervous wrecks, thinking, 'Please don't make a mistake that could cost us.' It was horrendous. We were abysmal.

So now we're in League One, the third tier. I was devastated. I'd been part of two relegations and losing so many football matches drains you. I'd sit at home some evenings and just think about it all. It wasn't as if I had a family to concentrate on or to take my mind off the football.

But just as losing had been a habit for some of my time at Norwich, winning became a habit in that League One season under Lambert. And that winning momentum was probably why Norwich did so well the next year and the one after that, going straight through the Championship and having a tremendous season in the Premier League.

But I left at the end of the League One season. I was in the team of the year selected by other players in the division, I was second in the Norwich Player Of The Season, but I sort of knew I wouldn't be staying. There was a clause in my contract that it could be extended for another year, but to trigger it, the club had to tell me by a certain date. That date came and went, and Lambert hadn't said anything to me so I guessed he was going to get new people in for the Championship. But I was enjoying the season so much that I honestly didn't worry about what would come next. Plus, I knew I'd been playing well and that other teams would want me, so there was no stress.

After all the celebrations, he called the players who were out of contract in individually. When he talked to me there was some general football chat, and I wondered if he was going to get round to telling me his decision about me. But eventually he made it obvious he was going to take the team in a new direction, without me. I would have liked to stay, because I knew the club was on the up, but it wasn't to be.

I was OK because I'd already had numerous offers, and I had no problem at all with Lambert because he'd been big enough to call me back into the fold and give me such a great season.

When I think back to my Norwich days now, there was a lot more good memories than bad. There were too many relegations while I was there, definitely, but I played through a real tough time for the club, when they had money problems and other clubs were spending big. I would have liked to be a younger player when Lambert arrived, with more of my best days ahead of me. I would have liked to have left Norwich where I joined them, in the Premier League, but I'd been part of the redemption, the rebirth, and that was very special.

I enjoyed a good rapport with the fans at Norwich, and seeing them and hearing them at some of the away games that season in League One will stay with me. I remember their reaction when I got two goals at Yeovil in the league, for instance. It was December, before we'd really climbed the table into the top two. Yeovil scored in the first half, but we were kicking towards our fans in the second half and Chrissy Martin equalised after about an hour. Then I made it 2-1 to us, but they equalised a couple of minutes later and then made it 3-2 in the

last minute. But in added time I popped up with my second
goal of the game to win us a point and our fans went absolutely
mad. Great days. Good memories. And, as I say, I have plenty
of them from my Norwich days.

I had a few offers when I left, and chose Charlton because that
gave me the chance to return to London and they sold me a story
about their ambitions. I had two seasons there, and they were
promoted at the end of the second one, but I was disappointed
with the number of games I was getting and, before the end of
the second season, I went on loan to Wycombe. The move was
made permanent that summer. Gary Waddock was Wycombe
manager and he was my captain at Luton.

After him, the job went to Gareth Ainsworth, who was the
other senior player alongside me in terms of age and experience,
and I loved playing for him. I was captain and Wycombe was
another club where I had a good relationship with the fans.

But I kept getting injuries. I had a back operation, I broke
an arm, and it was one thing after another. The final nail in
the coffin was that I damaged my knee in the last pre-season
game before the 2014-15 campaign. It didn't feel too bad, and
I played on for another ten minutes, and then an opponent
fell on it and did some more damage. I had done my posterior
cruciate ligament, torn my meniscus and made a right mess of
the whole joint.

I was laid up for a couple of months and it became clear
that I wasn't going to come back from that one. At Christmas
time, the team were doing really well, and I said to Gareth,
'Look, just cancel my contract so that you have a few more
quid to spend and keep this group together.' So that was what
happened. They lost in the play-off final but I know what I did
was the right thing. I didn't want to keep taking their money
when I was completely crocked.

Now I have done my coaching badges and I want to work in America. I love the country and I want to have a couple of years there. I enjoy coaching and passing on some of the things I learned. You never know, I might help some tall kid decide whether he's a defender or a striker.

Gary Doherty played for Norwich between 2004 and 2010, making 202 appearances and scoring 10 goals. He played under five managers and was the fans' Player Of The Season in 2005-06.

TALES FROM THE
CITY

Brilliant original stories about Norwich City FC
by journalists, fans and former players.

Tales From The City Volume 1

A collection of 11 stories about Norwich City
written by people who all have one thing in
common: a deep affinity with the club.

Compiled and edited by national newspaper
journalist Mick Dennis — a home-and-away
season-ticket holder — the first volume of
Tales From The City includes contributions
from Bryan Gunn, Michael Wynn Jones, Iwan
Roberts, Grant Holt, Paul McVeigh, Simon
Thomas, Chris Goreham, Charlie Wyett, Lilie
Ferrari, Jon Rogers and Mick Dennis.

Tales From The City Volume 2

The second volume of original writing about
the Canaries features chapters from former
players and managers as well as broadcasters
and journalists.

Editor Mick Dennis has assembled a stellar
cast of contributors including Ed Balls, Kevin
Bond, Karen Buchanan, Adam Drury, Darren
Eadie, Robert Fleck, Craig Fleming, Ruel Fox,
Malcolm Robertson, Keith Skipper, and Dave
Stringer.

All books in the series are available now from
www.talesfrom.com